THEN & NOW

THE SWANAGE BRANCH

ANDREW P. M. WRIGHT

THEN
&
NOW

THE SWANAGE BRANCH

ANDREW P. M. WRIGHT

IAN ALLAN
Publishing

First published 1992

ISBN 0 7110 2046 9

© Andrew P. M. Wright 1992

Published by Ian Allan Ltd, Shepperton, Surrey; and printed by Ian Allan Printing Ltd at their works at Coombelands in Runnymede, England.

Front cover, top:
A spirited departure from Swanage station, in the swinging 1960s. On a fine summer evening, ex-LMS Ivatt 2-6-2T No 41314 double-heads a grimy Standard Class 4 locomotive past the Victorian signalbox with a train for Corfe Castle and Wareham. 81 years of steam traction ended just a few weeks later on 4 September 1966. By Christmas 1967, rationalisation by BR had eliminated the many tracks and sidings together with the signalbox — leaving one weed-ridden track and a station lingering on until the line's closure on New Year's Day, 1972. *Chris Phillips*

Front cover, bottom:
After 14 years of hard work by dedicated volunteers, Swanage station was restored to its former glory — and the sceptics proved very wrong. Great Eastern Railway 'N7' class 0-6-2T No 69621 of 1924 waits to leave with an afternoon train for Herston and Harman's Cross in May 1990. Just 15 years before, everything seen here had gone — except for the derelict and boarded up station buildings. But Swanage Railway volunteers rebuilt and brought in the entire infrastructure needed to run and maintain a railway. The rest is history. *Andrew P. M. Wright*

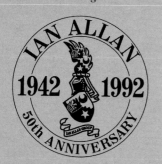

Contents

Acknowledgements   5

Preface   6

Introduction   12

ONE — The Ganger's Tale   18

TWO — The Wartime Porter's Tale   27

THREE — The American GIs' Tale   39

FOUR — The Wartime Fireman's Tale   44

FIVE — The Fireman's Tale   52

SIX — The Branch Driver's Tale   59

SEVEN — The Main Line Driver's Tale   66

EIGHT — The Signalman's Tale   72

NINE — The Area Manager's Tale   81

TEN — The Campaigner's Tale   89

ELEVEN — The Railwaymen's Tale   97

TWELVE — The Councillor's Tale   101

THIRTEEN — The Angry Young Man's Tale   105

FOURTEEN — The Prodigal Fireman's Tale   114

FIFTEEN — The Volunteer's Tale   121

Acknowledgements

Many generous people have graciously and selflessly helped me over the years. I would like to thank each one of them for their friendship, hospitality and infinite patience under persistent questioning and inquisitiveness on my part.

To the many photographers, I would like to thank them for their help and co-operation in going through their mountains of negatives — often in search of the most unusual picture of the Swanage branch. I also owe a big debt of gratitude to every ex-member of Swanage branch staff that I have talked to over the years for their time and hospitality. It is not easy, or enjoyable, to spend your valuable spare time talking about a working lifetime — especially when there are better things to do. But, they did.

Sincere thanks must also go to the locomotive crews and other operating staff on the Swanage Railway for their help and patience during my years of picture taking. My shout of 'Just one more please', has gone down into Swanage Railway folklore — always prompting a grin — and is the cause of many jokes.

The following deserve special mention for their kindness and assistance: Mike Arlett, Gerry Andrews, Hugh Ballantyne, Steve Barker, Edwin Bird, John Bird, Les Boyland, Librarians Kate Brennan and Michaela Horsfield of the *Evening Echo*, Bournemouth, Cliff and Eddy Brown, Stan Brown, Colin Caddy, David Cash, Henry Casserley, John Coleman, Moyra and Roger Cross, the late Derek Cross, Steve Dadd, Peter Downer, Peter Duncalfe, Mike and David Esau, Frank Farwell, Peter Frost, John Spencer-Gilks, Andrew Goltz, Dorothy Gossling, Arthur Grant, Bryan Green, David Haysom, William 'Taffy' Hazell, Les Hayward, Ken Hordle, Jimmy Hunt, Bob Inman, Handel Kardas, Frank Kitcatt, Brian Kohring of the Wimborne Railway Club for access to his collection of Swanage branch tickets; John Lakey, Rodney Lissenden, Alan Mabey, Paul McDonald, Arthur Meehan, Rae Montgomery, George Moon, David Morgan, Paddy Mulqueen, Sid Nash, Alan Norman, Fred Norman, Mel and Geraldine Norris, the late Ivo Peters, Chris Phillips, Bob Richards, Gerald Siviour, Doug Scott, John Scrace, Keith Sloper, David M. Smith, Mike Smith, Mike Standhaft, Tim Stephens, Mike Stollery, Mick Stone, Lens of Sutton, Peter Sykes, Stan Symes, Mervyn Turvey, Martyn Thresh, Tony Trood, Frank Waddington, Johnny Walker, Harold Ward, Albert Weekes, George Willey, and Raymond Wright.

Special thanks also to Eddy and Shelagh Spink, Steve and Michelle Bennett as well as Andy and Simon Spenceley — all of the Dorset Branch of the Military Vehicle Conservation Group for their help and technical advice.

Personal thanks must go to World War 2 GIs of the 26th Infantry Regiment, First Division — the 'Big Red One' — of the United States Army, for their memories of the Swanage branch at war from the other side of the Atlantic: William M. Lee, Mount Vernon, Illinois; Bill Costello, Detroit, Michigan; Danny D'Allesandro, Brooklyn, New York; Richard Beihl, Temple, Pennsylvania; Warren Coffman, Winter Springs, Florida; Jon Babyak, Mc Keesport, Pennsylvania; Marlin Brockette, Austin, Texas; James Foore, Tonawanda, New York; Alden Peckham, Freeport, Maine and Jack Gray, Arvada, Colorado.

I would also like to acknowledge the generous help of several newspapers for allowing me to quote from their publications: William Newman, Managing Editor of *The Sun*; Gareth Weekes, Editor of the *Evening Echo*, Bournemouth; Phil Pledger, Editor of the *Western Gazette*, Yeovil, and Cliff Moore, Editor of the *Advertiser* Series based in Poole, for old copies of the *Swanage Times*.

A big vote of thanks must also go to my long-time photographic printer, Derek Long, of Haviland Photo Sales in Bournemouth, for his skill, speed and patience in getting the best from negatives as deadlines loomed.

Preface

'It's like the Channel Tunnel project. You'll never see it in this century or ever — a lot of rubbish, all of it.'

Swanage resident, April 1975

With the reassuring comfort of hindsight it is now easy to scoff and snigger, but in the mid-1970s it was anybody's guess whether the Swanage Railway would even gain a foothold at the disused Victorian seaside station, let alone relay tracks the 6½ miles to Corfe Castle and beyond to link up with the British Rail network at Norden.

Back in 1972 the majority of the public and railway enthusiasts — and even some of the volunteers then clamouring to be allowed to rebuild the branch line — thought that completely relaying the Swanage Railway through the beautiful Purbeck region of southeast Dorset was a pipe dream.

However, the volunteers wanted to have a go. Then, if they failed, they would at least have the consolation of knowing that they had tried their best and that it really was impossible.

It was not; they succeeded against all the odds — physical, political and financial — and proved the doubting Jonahs very wrong. Through determined effort and almost missionary zeal, the volunteers of the Swanage Railway — young and old and from every conceivable background — have proved their point with rails, sleepers, locomotives, carriages and endless hard work.

Through their selfless efforts, personal and financial sacrifices, the volunteers have dragged sceptical local authorities, tourist boards and even British Rail's Network SouthEast round to their way of thinking; that the Swanage Railway is viable and does have a valuable and important role to play in the realms of tourism, transport and reducing the area's chronic summer traffic congestion problems.

The Swanage Railway is living proof that miracles can and do happen. In the words of early 1970s Birmingham University student, Andrew Goltz — the young man who formed the Swanage Railway Society back in 1972: 'The incredible thing was that we seemed to surmount every conceivable problem against all the odds — and not only come through

unscathed but emerge stronger than ever before to fight the next battle.'

Railways centre round the characters that enable them to run and the people who use them. In *The Swanage Branch Then and Now* there are 15 revealing tales from 15 very different people who knew the Swanage branch 'then' and 'now' — from 1929 right up to the present.

The range is diverse — from a young American GI for whom the branch line was an unexpected reminder of home and a valuable link with normality in the tense days before D-Day in June 1944, through to the 15-year-old porter for whom working at Swanage station was an 'education' that changed him from a boy to a man.

There is the track ganger who worked on the 10-mile branch line for nearly 45 years — tending the track with loving care — only to watch it being unceremoniously torn up with a JCB mechanical digger in just five weeks in the summer of 1972.

According to a signalman, his 19 years working at Corfe Castle and Swanage were the happiest working days of his life and he was literally 'worried sick' at the thought of leaving, when Swanage station was 'rationalised' and his signalbox abolished in 1967.

For the BR manager — who spent nearly 50 years working for the Southern Railway and then British Rail, only to be charged with closing the alleged loss-making Swanage branch — there was the irony of watching the line re-emerge and gain the support of British Rail 20 years after it had controversially closed the branch.

There is the branch fireman who had to tolerate his driver religiously quoting long passages from the Bible on the footplate; and the veteran driver who first worked to Swanage in the early 1940s and retired from BR in 1987 after driving over one and a half million miles — only to return to Swanage to drive steam locomotives in his spare time!

Find out about the stubbornness of an angry young man who gave birth to the Swan-

Above:

Living up to his reputation of always being seen in his grimy cap, with an oilcan and rag at hand, senior Swanage branch train driver Jack Spicer oils the motion of a 1940s LMS 2-6-2T Ivatt tank steam locomotive at Wareham's south bay, platform 1, between hauling trains down to Corfe Castle and Swanage in 1966. Starting his railway career in Kent between the wars, Jack moved to Swanage in the early 1940s and retired at the end of branch steam in 1966. *Chris Phillips*

age Railway — and the campaigner who moved to Swanage in a desperate attempt to save her daughter's life in 1945. Nineteen years later, her husband was the first to speak out after he suspected that the branch line was being run down a full eight years before it closed.

Included are the railwaymen who had the courage to speak out as their line died and the vociferous local councillor who spent over five years trying to prove that British Rail's alleged losses were false. He alleged to the

end that the line was killed off by a Civil Service formula devised in London.

For a young cleaner who started with British Railways in Bournemouth at the age of 15, the wheel has turned full circle — thanks to the Swanage Railway. Working down to Corfe Castle and Swanage as a fireman in the late 1950s before leaving BR, he was to return to Swanage in the 1990s as a volunteer fireman with a fellow ex-cleaner from over 30 years before.

The Victorian 'M7' tank locomotives may have delighted the hearts of many enthusiasts watching from the lineside fence in the 1950s and 1960s, but what were they like to work on? A long-time driver gives the insider's view, and why was a legendary driver so embarrassed that he was forced to hide his passenger train?

In *The Swanage Branch Then and Now* you will find out about how an anonymous 'deep throat' blew the whistle on British Rail and humorously signed himself '003 and a half' — and how a branch fireman came face to face with General Montgomery during the tense preparations for the massive and costly D-Day Allied invasion of France in June 1944.

What was it like for a young porter to experience the excitement of boarding General Eisenhower's personal train at Swanage station? How did a fireman escape death at the

Right:

Flashback to the Swanage branch at war. Ex-porter Albert Weekes takes a nostalgic trip back to the bitter-sweet days of 1943/1944 at Swanage station — in 1991. Albert joined the Southern Railway in 1943 at the age of 14 and experienced the friendly 'invasion' of American GIs during the tense days before D-Day. With Albert from left to right are 'Yanks' Simon Spenceley, Steve Bennett and Andrew Spenceley of the Dorset branch of the Military Vehicle Conservation Group. *Andrew P. M. Wright*

Above:
Standard Class 4 2-6-4T locomotive No 80032 glides past Swanage station's engine shed and turntable with the 09.50 branch train from Wareham on Monday 23 May 1966. In tow are two 1940s Bulleid carriages; built for main line express service, they were transferred for branch line work in Purbeck during 1965. The 1950s-designed Standard tank locomotives worked between Wareham and Swanage from 1963 until the end of branch steam on Monday 5 September 1966.
John Scrace

Left:
Just six years later, the scene at Swanage had changed radically. Steam had gone and the station 'rationalised' with only one track remaining, the engine shed closed and the turntable cut up for scrap. Sporting the '98' branch headcode, 1960s-built BR Crompton Class 33 diesel-electric No 6580 (later 33119) trundles into Swanage with the 09.55 train from London Waterloo on Saturday 23 August 1969. *Sid C. Nash*

hands of the Luftwaffe one May afternoon? Find out about the schoolboy's treasured dream that came true after he refused to take 'no' for an answer.

After starting to rebuild the Swanage branch from nothing but a few scrounged rails and sleepers in 1976, the volunteers are now on target to connect up with the BR network at Norden. They reached the one-mile point at Herston on the outskirts of Swanage in 1984, the three-mile point at Harman's Cross in 1989 and finally the five-mile point at Corfe Castle station in 1990.

The financial crisis that exploded in shocked members' faces early in 1991 was the Swanage Railway's toughest test but yet another hurdle in the Project's long history that very nearly could have rendered it extinct.

From Corfe, it is just three-quarters of a mile to the site of the Swanage Railway's halt and car park between Norden and Corfe Cas-

tle — and just three-quarters of a mile beyond that to the BR network.

After the General Manager of BR's Southern Region, Gordon Pettitt, opened the Swanage Railway's new Harman's Cross station in March 1989, BR Network SouthEast is now waiting to welcome the Swanage Railway when they link up between Norden and Furzebrook.

BR management has said that it would like to see Swanage Railway trains run again through to Wareham station — something that last happened on New Year's Day 1972.

In the words of the high-powered director of BR's Network SouthEast, Chris Green, who wrote to Swanage Railway Co Chairman, David Cash, after a fact-finding mission to the rebuilt railway in December 1989: 'You are performing miracles as you narrow the gap between Harman's Cross and Furzebrook. My overriding impression is one of professional teamwork by people who are enjoying

their work'. He added: 'The visit reconfirmed my belief that the greatest commercial value to both parties now lies in a steam operation into the "up" bay platform at Wareham.'

The Swanage Branch Then and Now is a tribute to the triumph of the human spirit when faced with a variety of challenges and pressures — during the good times and the bad — as well as the people that worked on Purbeck's railway 'then' and continue to toil 'now'. With the aid of stirring and evocative photographs from across the years, this book will make you feel a part of the Swanage branch line, as though you actually experienced it.

Finally, this book is dedicated to two very special people, now sadly passed away but still greatly missed — Christian Forsyth and Stuart Gray.

Andrew P. M. Wright,
Tarrant Keyneston
Dorset
August 1991

Facing page, top:
Stripped of all vestages of a railway, Swanage station stands desolate one bright but cold winter's afternoon in 1977. The Victorian engine shed — last used in 1966 — stands disused with the turntable pit full of water. No train has run here for five years but Swanage Railway Society volunteers have already laid a tiny piece of track by the old coaling dock where an ex-Southern Railway scenery van is standing. The first public trains over just a few hundred yards of track were not to run for another three years. *David R. Morgan*

Facing page, bottom:
Just four years later, the scene had changed dramatically and the embryonic Swanage Railway taken hold of the station site. With a main line and headshunt tracks laid by hand — and rusting steam locomotives rescued from Barry Docks scrapyard in South Wales for restoration — oil-burning, built in 1954, Barclay 0-4-0ST steam locomotive *Richard Trevithick* slowly hauls two restored carriages the few hundred yards from the engine shed to the station on Sunday 7 September 1980. *Tim Hengst*

Left:
With the impending end of steam traction after 81 years, a brave new 1960s British Rail image comes to Swanage station. Porter/shunter George Symes (left) and porter Bill 'Taffy' Hazell sport their new uniforms outside the station's parcels office in the summer of 1966. Both George and Bill worked at Swanage until the branch was closed on Monday 3 January 1972. Tragically, George died just six months later, as the country branch line that was his life was being torn up for scrap. *Chris Phillips*

Introduction

'Thanks to the directors of the new railway . . . Swanage will be united with England. We hope this praiseworthy enterprise for the convenience of the public will meet with merited support.'
Wareham and Isle of Purbeck Advertiser, 17 October 1884.

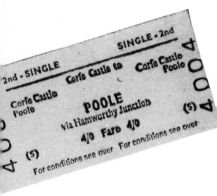

It took almost 40 years to persuade the Isle of Purbeck's Victorian landed gentry of the merits of a Swanage branch line connecting them with London; nearly two years to construct it in time for the grand opening in May 1885 — but just under six weeks to tear it all up for scrap during the hot summer of 1972.

Mirroring the entrepreneurs' weary battle of a century before, the early 1970s saw the start of an incredible 18-year fight to completely rebuild the infrastructure needed to run and maintain a railway at Swanage — and relay the five miles of track required to reach Corfe Castle in 1990.

The first scheme for a 10-mile railway to connect the emerging Dorset seaside resort of Swanage with the Medieval village of Corfe Castle and the market town of Wareham came in 1847. It was planned as a branch off the then new Southampton & Dorchester main line from London — the proposed line serving the stone quarries around Swanage. A second attempt in 1861 by the London & South Western Railway Co (LSWR) aimed at serving the ball clay mines around Creech, Furzebrook and Norden between Corfe Castle and Wareham. It also failed. The landowning gentry of the area did not approve.

The Isle of Purbeck Railway Co, supported by the LSWR, tried to promote a line to serve the area in 1862 with a plan broadly along the lines of the 1847 one. However, local protests

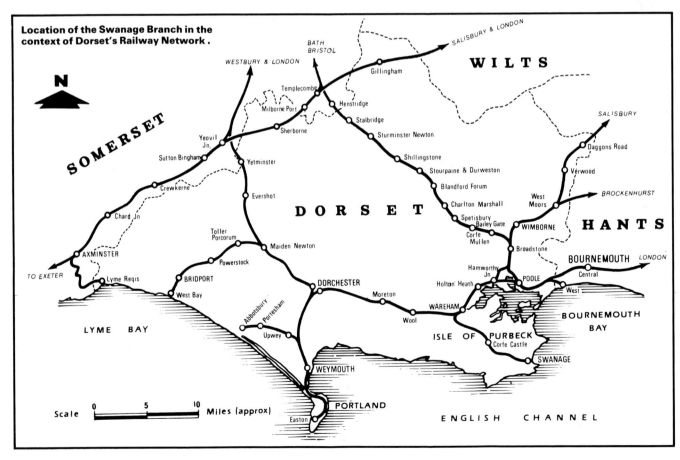

over the severing of Wareham's ancient Iron Age walls slowly suffocated it.

Swanage entrepreneur and quarry owner George Burt — the 'father' of the emerging seaside resort — joined forces with businessman John Mowlem, founder of the world-famous construction company. Together, they tried to link Swanage and Corfe Castle with the outside world in 1877. Two routes were proposed; one passing close to Wareham's western walls before running through the village of Stoborough then on to Furzebrook, Corfe and Swanage.

The second route went completely round the problem by leaving the main London to Weymouth line one and a half miles west of Wareham station at the tiny hamlet of Worgret. The line would then run across the heaths to the clay mines at Furzebrook and Norden before running down to Corfe Castle and Swanage.

Delighted with their ingenious alternative routes, the two Victorian gentlemen thought they had cracked it. They employed the professional services of the LSWR's consulting engineer, Mr Galbraith of Messrs Galbraith & Church. His authority swung the day and the local gentry finally came round to supporting the idea of a branch line connecting them with London.

The parliamentary Swanage Railway Act permitting the construction of the new line passed through the House of Commons and then the Lords before being signed by Queen Victoria on Thursday 8 July 1881.

Just under two years later construction of the line began at Swanage, on Friday 5 June 1883. The promoters set themselves the target of completing the line in under two years and spending £76,646 in the process.

Curry & Reeves of Westminster were contracted to build the line between Swanage and Corfe Castle with Bull & Co of Southampton building Corfe and Swanage stations out of Purbeck stone. E. G. Perkins of Lymington in Hampshire were sub-contracted to build the two iron viaducts over the River Frome near Worgret Junction as well as the five-mile stretch of line from the junction down to Corfe Castle.

After the first steam locomotive — a brand-new Beattie well tank — was hauled from Wareham down to Swanage by a team of 42 carthorses in a delicate day-long operation, it triumphantly hauled the first passenger train up to Corfe Castle and Wareham on Wednesday 20 May 1885 — an auspicious day declared a public holiday in the Purbecks. The first train left the new Swanage station at 07.20, reached Corfe Castle at 07.30 before

Right:

Just before a summer shower, Victorian 'M7' 0-4-4T locomotive No 30108 wheezes asthmatically and leaks steam as she pushes her two-coach afternoon 'push-pull' train from Wareham to Swanage during the first week of August 1963. In the cab at the far end of the two-coach Maunsell carriage set, the train driver is about to collect the single-line key token from the signalman as the train swings left, off the London to Weymouth main line, and on to the Swanage branch proper.
John R. Woolley

Centre right:

Twenty-eight years later, a five-coach hi-tech British Rail Class 442 'Wessex Electric' speeds past Worgret Junction with the 12.32 London Waterloo to Weymouth train on Saturday 29 June 1991. Clay workings and gas trains for BP's Wytch Farm on-shore oil field are the only workings to now use the surviving three-mile stub of the old Swanage branch. Worgret Junction signalbox was abolished on Sunday 23 May 1976, and replaced with an open five-lever ground frame.
Andrew P. M. Wright

Below right:

Hordes of railway enthusiasts scramble to get a picture of 'West Country' class unrebuilt Bulleid Pacific No 34023 *Blackmore Vale* at Corfe Castle station between rain showers on Sunday 7 May 1967. The special 10-coach 'Dorset Coast Express' railtour ran down from London, was one of the final steam trains to run in the Isle of Purbeck and was organised by the Locomotive Club of Great Britain. The branch line was so popular that the long train made two trips down to Swanage for the benefit of enthusiasts from all over the country. *John H. Bird*

The end of the line for the Swanage branch. It's the first week of August 1972, and scrapmen from Eagre & Co of Scunthorpe are tearing up the branch track. An enthusiast helplessly looks on at the scene of desecration and sheer depression. Two open wagons and a flat wagon stand on the 'down' line, filled with lifted rails, chairs and track bolts. Behind the wagons, the starting signal has been stripped of its enamel arm.
Gerry Andrews

Centre left:
Fifteen years after the tracks at Corfe Castle were torn up for scrap, nature has taken over and it's hard to believe that long 10-coach London trains carrying excited holidaymakers once simmered here before leaving for Swanage. Looking towards Wareham on Saturday 4 July 1987, the old goods yard lies deep amongst choking weeds to the left, with two rescued Victorian carriage bodies placed on the trackbed by the Swanage Railway.
Andrew P. M. Wright

Below left:
Appearances can be deceptive and four years later, the choking undergrowth at Corfe Castle has been cut back. Here on Tuesday 11 September 1990, Swanage Railway volunteers relay the tracks at the station — 18 years after the final BR train trundled into the passing loop at Corfe Castle station from Swanage on New Year's Day 1972. Although the volunteers seen here have the assistance of a 15-ton diesel-electric crane to lay the 60ft track panels, the first mile of track at Swanage was laboriously laid by hand using an old GWR hand crane.
Andrew P. M. Wright

Above:

The typical branch line scene. Victorian 'M7' 0-4-4T tank locomotive No 30052 simmers at the head of its two-coach 'push-pull' Maunsell set at Swanage before departing for Corfe Castle and Wareham on Sunday 19 May 1963. Beyond the stopblocks to the left are the gables of the 'Railway Hotel'. 'M7' No 30052 had worked the Swanage branch since the previous April, moving to Bournemouth MPD from Yeovil. She was scrapped with her other Purbeck sisters at Briton Ferry, Glamorgan, in October 1964.

John Spencer-Gilks/Ryedale AV

departing one minute later. Excited Victorian passengers trundled past Worgret Junction signalbox at 07.40 before running into Wareham at 07.45. Goods trains started running on 1 June 1885.

Operated by the LSWR from the start, the Swanage branch line came under the control of the Southern Railway with the grouping of Britain's railway companies into the 'Big Four' on New Year's Day 1923. World War 2 proved a challenge for the branch — as with all the country's railways — and while the Purbecks recovered from six years of war, the Swanage line came under British Railways with the Labour Government's nationalisation in January 1948. Everything continued as normal through the 1950s, scarcely changed since the heyday of the Swanage branch line in the 1920s and 1930s. With the advent of the motor car, road traffic was competing fiercely with the railways — and winning. The early 1960s saw the line undergo a series of painful changes. Timetables were altered and the first major service change on the Swanage branch came with the withdrawal of its through-carriages on the prestigious 'Royal Wessex' service from Weymouth to London. Lord Beeching's infamous report on the railways was published in March 1963, and by the autumn of that year, Purbeck lost its Sunday

trains in the winter. Freight services were suspended on Monday 4 October 1965. Local people feared the worst and railway enthusiasts descended on the picturesque Dorset branch line in ever-increasing numbers as steam traction approached the end of its 81-year reign. Steam finally expired on the morning of Monday 5 September 1966, when a modern diesel unit took over; the timetable was changed and the services reduced. Corfe Castle and Swanage stations were rationalised during 1967 and 1968. Closure was announced in 1969 when the last timetabled through-train ran to Poole, Bournemouth and London. From October 1969, branch passengers had to change for main line trains at Wareham. But, the expected closure did not take place, until, after repeated reprieves and swings in local morale amongst railway supporters and passengers, the final train ran from Swanage up to Corfe Castle and Wareham on the cold evening of 1 January 1972. Six months later — amidst loud howls of protest from local people — the tracks were torn up for scrap and the Victorian stations boarded up to await an unknown fate at the hands of greedy developers. Purbeck thought it had lost its railway forever. That was not to be the end. An even more remarkable story was to follow.

Left:
Swanage station in 1976, two years after society volunteers saved the Victorian station from the bulldozer and gained access to the boarded-up building after a four-year battle. The platform was demolished in July 1974, after the town council purchased the site the previous March. No tracks have been laid into the station yet but volunteers have made a start on restoring the platform canopy. *Peter Sykes*

Below left:
Nearly 300 years worth of Victorian locomotives stand at the restored station on the summer evening of Friday 22 May 1987. 1897-designed 'M7' 0-4-4T No 30053 worked the Swanage branch during her last month of active service with BR in April 1964. In 1987, No 30053 made a triumphant return to Swanage from the USA thanks to the Drummond Locomotive Preservation Society. To the left is LSWR 'B4' 0-4-0T No 96 *Normandy*, of 1893, from the Bluebell Railway in Sussex. Behind the 'B4' is Midland Railway '1F' 0-6-0T locomotive 41708, built in 1880. *Andrew P. M. Wright*

The Ganger's Tale

1

'Track work was hard in those days because we didn't have the machinery that British Rail does now. If we were on a relaying job there would be eighty men working by hand — crowbarring sleepers and rails off the back of the train.'

Edwin Bird

Below:
A familiar scene which many thought would last forever. With the driver enjoying the sunshine, LSWR Adams 'T1' class 0-4-4T locomotive No E67 pauses while running round its two-coach train at Swanage before departing for Corfe Castle and Wareham on the warm summer morning of Sunday 6 July 1930. First helping to run the 'push-pull' train service in Purbeck from 1925, the Drummond 'M7' 0-4-4Ts continued until May 1964. From then until September 1966, BR Standard tanks and LMS Ivatt tanks took over the mantle.
Henry Casserley

It was the solitary and claustrophobic confines of a beautiful but lonely walled garden in a quiet west Dorset village that forced a 20-year-old man to leave his job as a gardener — suddenly packing his bags and moving across the county to Swanage in 1928.

Now, over 60 years later, and nearly two decades after retiring from British Rail, 83-year-old Edwin Bird is still gardening — tending the flower beds outside the small terraced house in Swanage that he moved into with his wife back in 1936. For his 45 years on the railways, 44 of them as a track ganger on the Swanage branch line, Eddy has only a couple of faded black and white photos tucked away in a drawer — but a lifetime full of memories. Most of the Dorset characters he worked with, and who would now seem to have come from a different world, have sadly died.

After arriving in Swanage in 1928, desperate for a job, he had a spell working at the stone quarries in nearby Langton Matravers.

Above:
A rare view of the Swanage track gang by the 'up' home signal at Corfe Castle station during World War 2. From left to right are: Frank King, Edwin Bird, Alfie Crabb and Ted Bartlett. The picture was taken by a track ganger who won a Brownie camera after saving up cards from packets of 'Craven A' cigarettes which cost just sixpence for a pack of 20! *Courtesy of Edwin Bird*

Left:
Smiles all round from Swanage Railway volunteers nearly half a century later. A marathon track-laying effort in April 1990, pushed the Purbeck Line over half a mile from Harman's Cross towards Corfe Castle in just 10 days. With the medieval castle in view from the railhead for the first time, the track gang take a break under the A351 Afflington road bridge on Tuesday 10 April 1990 — 18 years after the BR track was lifted at the same spot in July 1972. *Andrew P. M. Wright*

Right:
Long 10-coach trains once accelerated through here, packed with excited holidaymakers in peacetime — and crammed with apprehensive young men bound for the battlefields in war. The 1 in 80 descent into Corfe Castle station from Swanage lies desolate and invaded with choking undergrowth on the morning of Thursday 17 May 1990. The medieval ruins of the castle dwarf the Victorian station buildings, built by Bull & Co of Southampton in 1884 and sporting 18in thick walls of Purbeck stone.
Andrew P. M. Wright

Below:
Six months later, the same scene had changed totally and the railway returned to Corfe Castle. On Wednesday 10 October 1990, ex-BR 0-6-0 Class 08 diesel shunter, No D3591, from 1958 stands with an engineering train during 'Exercise Topham Hatt Two'. The special 10-day exercise involved members of the Royal Corps of Signals from Northern Ireland installing lineside telephone poles, cables and a telephone exchange between Harman's Cross and Corfe Castle stations. *Andrew P. M. Wright*

He also helped to erect and dismantle the large annual Territorial Army summer camps just outside Swanage.

One day, the gardener's son heard of a job going on the town's railway. He applied for it and joined the Southern Railway in September 1929. His first day as a track ganger was spent digging holes for new fence posts at Harman's Cross — close to where the Swanage Railway was to build its new station over 60 years later. In contrast, his final day with British Rail in February 1973 was spent working with Wareham's mobile track gang on the other side of their 'patch' at East Stoke level crossing between Worgret junction and Wool. During his 45-year working career on Purbeck's railway, Eddy Bird put in more than 112,000 hours carefully tending the Swanage branch track.

'We used to cut the grass on both sides of the track all the way from Swanage to Wareham then. Now it's just a load of overgrown

Above left:
The Corfe-based track gang that tended the five-mile Corfe to Worgret Junction section received an award from BR's Southern Region for the quality of their work in 1950. Here on Wednesday 31 May 1950, the Southern Region's chief permanent way engineer from Eastleigh presents gang leader Alfie Allingham with a certificate by the A351 Catseye Bridge at Norden. From left to right are Walter Burden, Ken Andrews and Sid Stickland with the area's permanent way inspector Arch Rendell standing, with his spirit level, on the far right. Ken remembers 40 years on: 'I got £5 — quite something when we were then only on £7 or £8 a week.'
Photograph Courtesy of BR Southern Region/ Joan Brown collection

Left:
It's unbelievable but this is the spot that the Corfe track gang proudly received their award from BR on that May day in 1950 — but photographed 41 years later on the hot summer afternoon of Sunday 14 July 1991. Looking towards Furzebrook, birch trees, bracken and choking undergrowth have completely overwhelmed the trackbed just 19 years after the once-manicured track was torn up for scrap at this spot in late August 1972.
Andrew P. M. Wright

21

brambles and bushes,' remembers Edwin with a sad note of resignation in his voice.

The sprightly octogenarian, who looks like a man 20 years younger, had seen the Swanage branch thrive in the heydays of the 1920s and 1930s. He was there when it responded to the wartime challenge of the 1940s, experienced the new optimism of the 1950s before being forced to watch the branch's slow and inexorable decline through the 1960s which, some allege, led to the line's closure by starvation in 1972.

Born in Binghams Melcombe between the rural market towns of Dorchester and Blandford Forum on 11 February 1908 — when King Edward VII was on the throne — teenager Edwin spent six years working in the rural peace of a country garden at Sydling St Nicholas near Maiden Newton. The garden was too peaceful for the active young man — like solitary confinement. It was in the late summer of 1929, while the money and stock markets in London and New York were crashing, plummeting the western world into deep recession and forcing desperate stockbrokers to commit suicide — that Edwin heard there was a permanent way job going with the Southern Railway at Swanage. 'I saw Inspector Smith at Wareham, went to Southampton for the medical and eyesight test and got the job. I started off on 39 shillings and threepence (£1.96) a week, which was great compared with the £1 a week on the gardening. In 1930, my pay went up by one shilling.'

The names come flooding back as Eddy's mind searches back over 60 years. 'There was Mr Day, Mr Ierson, Mr Rendell and Stan Irwin. I started off as a lengthman on the New Barn to Corfe length, working with William Stockley from Harman's Cross and George Diffey from Langton Matravers.'

When Eddy joined the Southern Railway, the 10 miles of single track was placed in the hands of 14 men in four teams of gangers. Four gangers looked after the section from Swanage station up to New Barn. There, a team of three men took over and maintained the stretch up to the approaches to Corfe village and the 'up' distant signal by the common bridge. From there, through the station and as far as Furzebrook was the preserve of a four-man team. The final three-mile stretch, from the clay sidings up to Worgret Junction and the main line, was maintained by a three-man gang. But, by the 1930s, the gangs were merged with one six-man gang looking after the track from Swanage to Corfe Castle and another six-man gang tending the stretch from Corfe to Worgret Junction.

Eddy remembers a few names from over 30 years before: 'In the Swanage gang there was Alfie Crabb, George Farr, Burt Spicer, George Diffey, Bill Stockley and myself. It was in the early 1950s that John Coogan — who retired in 1990 — took the place of Alfie Crabb. Up at Corfe station there was Frank King, Bill Orchard, Gerry Welsh, and Alfie Allingham.'

The two gangs at Corfe and Swanage were to stay until 1967, when they were merged and moved to Wareham as a 'mobile' gang that worked on the main line as well as the branch. The changeover took place on Monday 24 April 1967, when their new 'empire' extended to Rockley Bridge, near Hamworthe, in the east and Winfrith in the west.

'Inspector Smith wasn't tough on us when I first joined,' recalls Eddy. 'None of the permanent way inspectors were really — they didn't drive you. As long as you did your work, that was it.'

The Swanage branch's track gangs would often be called to work on other parts of the system in Dorset such as the 'Old Road' to Ringwood and Brockenhurst in Hampshire; the cross-country route up to Salisbury and the old Somerset and Dorset main line up to Blandford Forum, Templecombe and Bath. Permanent way work, whether on the double-track main line or the single-track branch line in Purbeck, called for muscle and stamina.

'Track work was hard in those days, because we didn't have the machinery that the BR gangs have now. If we were on a relaying job, there would be eighty men working by hand — crowbarring sleepers and rails off the back of the train.

'I can clearly remember my first night relaying because it was the night that the new R101 airship blew up in France — Monday 6 October 1930. An awful rough, wild night it was. We were relaying a mile of track along the main line through Moreton by Woodsford — between Wool and Dorchester.

'We'd pull the old sleepers out of the ballast using long-handled tongs called sleeper dogs and then bar the new sleepers and the rails off the back of the train. We had to work by tilly lamps and during the war — because of the blackout — we had to work in the dark. After a while, we were able to see in the dark and, as any ganger will tell you, although it may appear dark at night, there is no such thing as complete darkness.'

Over 60 years on, Edwin Bird is glad he escaped the confines of the walled garden and joined the railways — despite the Swanage branch ending 43 years later in such widespread bitterness and resentment among its loyal staff. 'I've no regrets,' says Eddy. 'Work was scarce back in 1928 and, although the job was hard, once you learnt the work, it was bearable. There were rough times — the night time relaying jobs and spending all

LOVELY DORSET SANDS · SAFE BATHING
GUIDE FREE FROM TOWN HALL (DEPT. SR.) SWANAGE
EXPRESS TRAINS AND CHEAP FARES BY
SOUTHERN RAILWAY

Write for information to Town Hall (Dept. Y) Swanage

BRITISH RAILWAYS

night watching for slippage on the New Barn embankment between Harman's Cross and Swanage. But, you had to take the rough with the smooth — there's good and bad in every job. Nothing is ideal.'

Lengthmen Frank King and Bill Dorey were the branch line's regular patrolmen for many years. Frank would 'walk' the Worgret Junction to Corfe section checking for displaced keys or broken fishplates, while Bill would deal with the Corfe to Swanage section. The 1950s saw improvements in the branch track after much of it was relaid in 1947 to make up for arrears of the mid-1930s and during World War 2.

The long straight down to the Frome river — which ran at a gradient of 1 in 78 under Holme Lane bridge — was relaid on concrete sleepers in 1953, and in 1956 two further stretches were relaid. The first stretch to be upgraded was the one-and-a-half-mile length from Victoria Avenue bridge at Swanage — known to the gangers as 'gas house bridge' because of the nearby gas works sidings — through Herston and up towards New Barn. The second was the short run from Quarr Farm up the 1 in 76 gradient to Harman's Cross where the Swanage Railway would later build Dorset's first completely new station for over half a century, in 1988.

Back in the 1930s, Eddy Bird and the rest of the Swanage branch gangs were involved in a special permanent way experiment at Wareham station, when they laid a stretch of track on steel sleepers. By the late 1960s, three of Wareham's new 'mobile' gang walked both the main line and the withered arm down to Swanage. Cyril Tilly used to walk the stretch from Admiralty Bridge at Holton Heath down to Worgret Junction, while Fred Pitman walked from there to Wool. One man, Gerry Welsh, was charged with walking the 10 miles from Worgret Junction down to Corfe Castle and Swanage twice a week.

By the end of the Swanage branch line, Wareham's 'mobile' gang was made up of just 11 gangers: Stan Smith, Ted 'Edwin' Talbot, Tony Trood, Edwin Bird, Cyril Tilly, Charlie Bird, John Coogan, Arthur and Tom Stockley as well as Ken Ridout and Tom Biles.

Some gangers used to say that the branch was laid with 45ft long lengths of rail because that was the maximum length of rails that could be carried across the Atlantic to Britain on United States Liberty ships during World War 2.

Above:

Drowning out the quiet country station with a curious mixture of an electric whine and a loud diesel throb, the 600bhp diesel-electric engine of three-coach 'Hampshire' class DEMU No 1128 accelerates away from Corfe Castle station's 'down' platform with the 16.44 Wareham to Swanage train on Thursday 7 August 1969. First running on Monday 5 September 1966, the 'Hampshire' DEMUs operated the branch service until the last day on Saturday 1 January 1972. *John Scrace*

Right:

Nineteen years later, the deafening noise of a diesel train leaving Corfe Castle station for Swanage was just a fast-fading memory. The weed-choked platforms at Corfe stand silent on the evening of Sunday 7 August 1988. To the left is the old Unigate milk works which have been converted into small industrial units for local businesses. On the right is an overgrown pine tree in the old station master's garden. *Andrew P. M. Wright*

24

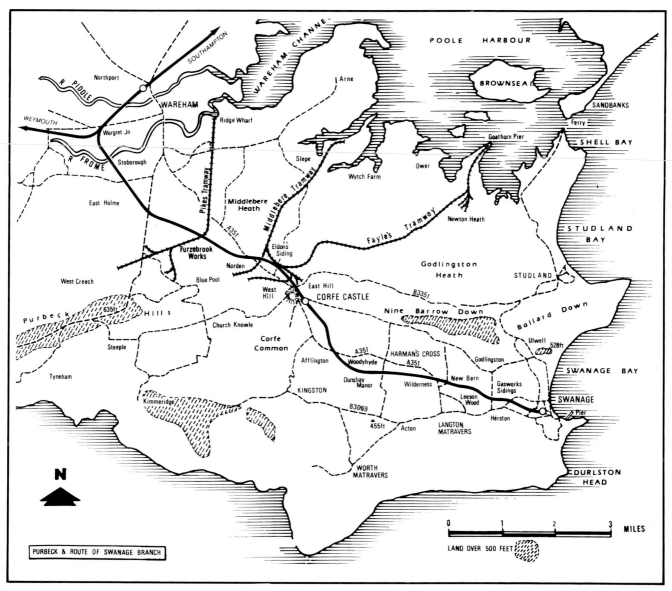

PURBECK & ROUTE OF SWANAGE BRANCH

LAND OVER 500 FEET

Even quite obscure parts of Edwin Bird's railway career come to the octogenarian's mind. He remembers replacing old wooden sleeper drains with new pre-cast concrete drain channelling in two places — on the line-side at Eldon's clay exchange siding in 1942 and later at Afflington Bridge in 1946. 'We only had two 60ft lengths of rail on the whole branch and they were at Afflington because we didn't have any 45ft lengths spare at the time.'

Eddy Bird reveals it was not the massive 'Battle of Britain' and 'West Country' class Bulleid Pacifics that damaged the track with their long London trains. Instead, it was the tiny 'M7' locomotives, with their two-coach LSWR 'Ironclad' and then finally Maunsell push-pull carriage sets, that were to blame. 'Some of the "M7s" used to travel quite fast, especially on the last train down from Wareham and Corfe Castle, when the crew wanted to get into the Railway Hotel by Swanage station for a drink. The "M7s" used to move the

track out of alignment because they were light on their feet and could get up to high speeds. We used to have six concrete sleepers under the Nursery Road bridge near New Barn to keep the track in gauge on the tight curve.'

As soon as World War 2 broke out, the railway's own Home Guard was formed in parallel with the one in Swanage town. 'Wareham and Swanage stations had their own Home Guard but Corfe came in with us at Swanage. We used to travel on the train to Wareham for our weekly training sessions in the goods yard there by the stationmaster's house on Thursday nights. We did rifle drill, marching and shooting and hand grenade practice before catching the last train back to Swanage.

'It was a serious business because we didn't know when the Germans were going to invade, but we did have some laughs as well. Every member of the Home Guard, which was everyone on the railway who was even reasonably medically fit, was supplied with a

25

M303 rifle and five rounds of ammunition, which they had to keep at home. In fact, Swanage station's team was so good with .22in rifles that they used to compete in shooting competitions held in what used to be the town's now-demolished Durlston Court Hotel.

'We'd also practice map reading at Swanage, be given lectures and rehearse gas mask procedures. We were even given lessons on how to use Sten guns and machine guns by members of the Grenadier Guards, who were billeted in Swanage at the beginning of the war.'

During the war, a large rail-mounted gun was set up on a siding on the north side of the branch track near the Motala Kennels at Norden. It was camouflaged with Cullacourt netting and the pine trees there. 'The gun was served by a locomotive and crew from Wareham and occasionally they took it out for practices. I heard they wanted to instal another gun further towards Corfe Castle at Eldon's Siding but this was never done.'

The huge 12in howitzer was set up by the 14th Super Heavy Battery, 5th Corps, during the autumn of 1940. The rail-mounted gun was served by a 'K10' class 4-4-0 locomotive No 393 from October of that year and was supplied by the Southern Railway.

In mid-February 1944, Eddy Bird and his fellow gangers were called in to guard the branch's farm crossings when special trains carrying Churchill, the King, Eisenhower and Montgomery ran down to Swanage. The dignitaries were in the Purbecks on Friday the 11th and Saturday February 12th, to watch vital sea and air practices at Studland beach for the D-Day Allied landings on the Normandy coast just four months later.

'I had to be on guard duty at a crossing between Herston and New Barn at 2am. Our instructions were not to let anyone cross the line. I waited for one of the trains to pass by before running back across the fields to my home at Herston — then being back at work at 7.12am the following morning.

'Eisenhower's train was in the main platform at Swanage, with the others in the bay platform and the goods yard. I'll always remember a large anti-aircraft gun that was positioned on Northbrook Road bridge to protect the station. The whole place was guarded by military policemen in their distinctive red caps.'

Looking back, Eddy Bird says the closure of the Swanage line alienated and frustrated the staff that worked on it — and was completely unnecessary.

'It should never have been closed. What they should have done was to remove some of the trains that were under-used, but still retain the morning, lunchtime and teatime trains. We were all surprised that the surplus tracks at Swanage were ripped up so quickly in the autumn of 1967. They were gone within two weeks or so.'

The man who spent nearly half a century maintaining the branch track — before watching it unceremoniously ripped up in just five weeks during the summer of 1972 — says he has been surprised and impressed at what the Swanage Railway volunteers have been able to achieve.

'I never thought the Swanage Railway would ever come back — never,' he admits. 'I thought the railway volunteers were completely wasting their time when they started at the station with a few rails and sleepers in the mid-1970s. I didn't think they had a hope in hell's chance of rebuilding the line.

'I think they'll get to Wareham eventually but I don't know if it will make any difference to the traffic queues between Swanage, Corfe and Wareham during the summer.

'Sometimes the old days on the branch seem like only yesterday and then at other times they seem like an age away. The mind plays funny tricks,' admits Eddy.

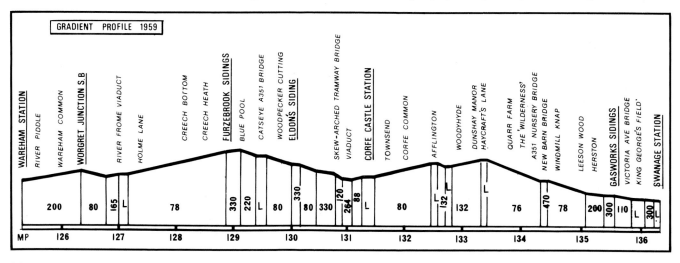

The Wartime Porter's Tale

2

'The American troops leaned out of the train windows as they left for D-Day. They were cheerful and gave me the thumbs up. I smiled and returned the gesture. I always wonder what happened to them and whether they came back.'

Albert Weekes

It is 1944 and 15-year-old junior porter Albert Weekes zips round Swanage station doing his daily chores between branch trains when he notices an American lad sat alone on one of the benches. In his smart dress uniform sporting the distinctive red badge of the 'Big Red One' — the crack First Division of the US Army — the young soldier is looking up and down the platform. Albert realises the GI has been sitting there for quite a time, the American's mind seemingly elsewhere.

Being a comparative youngster, and suspecting the soldier is homesick, Albert walks up to the young man and starts to make conversation. 'Are you all right, sir?' he asks hesitantly.

'Yep, OK, thanks, kid,' comes the confident answer.

'I've seen you before down here, haven't I?' adds the young junior porter as the GI gazes wistfully out across the tracks.

'Yep,' comes the answer.

From the twang and drawl of the soldier's accent, the young Albert realises that the American GI comes from the deep south of the United States.

'You like trains then?' asks Albert as he sits down on the bench beside the 'Yank'.

'Back home in the States we have a Southern Railway, too — the Alabama Great Southern Railroad Company,' the infantry-man replies. 'Comin' down here kind'a reminds me of the folks back home.'

The young junior porter did not know what to say — he felt sorry for the foreign soldier.

That is just one of Albert Weekes' vivid memories of his four years with the Southern Railway at Swanage — from the autumn of 1943 and the preparations for the D-Day Allied landings through to the coming of peace in the summer of 1945; before the slow adjustment as Swanage shed its drab, wartime colours and returned to its prewar status as a popular, family seaside resort in 1947. Had it not been for his mother determinedly doing the 'hard sell' on the youngster to Swanage's

formidable stationmaster, Mr Nobbs, then Albert Weekes would not have joined the Southern Railway in September 1943.

Had Mr Nobbs not agreed to take the young man on fresh from school then Albert would have not been given a special teenage insight into how the friendly 'invasion' of American GIs in November of that year affected Swanage station — along with the rest of the seaside town — as the south of England steadily and secretly prepared for the massive D-Day invasion of France. 'I always say joining the railway at Swanage educated me — I really enjoyed my time there. I joined as a boy in September 1943, and left a young man in 1947 to do my National Service with the Army,' says Albert, now a telephone engineer with British Telecom in Bournemouth and close to retirement.

Born and brought up in Swanage — the son of a builder's labourer — Albert went to the Herston School, which was almost within sight of the branch railway line.

Above:
A *déjà vu* feeling for ex-wartime porter at Swanage, Albert Weekes. In June 1991, he recreates the early morning in November 1943, when he saw his first American GIs arrive in Swanage to practice for the historic D-Day landings. 'Helping them off the train, I was struck how dark their faces were. They'd just taken part in the North Africa and Sicily landings', he remembers. Leaning from the 1930-built Southern Railway Maunsell carriage at Swanage in 1991 are modern-day US Army First Division GIs Simon and Andrew Spenceley of the Military Vehicle Conservation Group's Dorset branch. *Andrew P. M. Wright*

27

Right:
Still sporting its 1930s enamel signs — and scarcely changed since the 1940s — Swanage station is a hive of activity in the summer of 1969. But it's a station with less than three years to live. A three-coach 'Hampshire' DEMU, No 1128 disgourges its passengers after arriving at the terminus with the 13.13 from Corfe Castle and Wareham on Saturday 23 August 1969. Mrs Phyllis Cook's bookstall can be seen under the waiting room sign. Just three years after this picture was taken there would be no railway here at all.
John H. Bird

Below
Swanage's restored station in 1990, looking as though the railway was never taken away. The 1938 canopy has been fully restored, the platform cleared of tonnes of rubbish and rubble and the main line and run-round loop tracks relaid. Midland Railway '1F' 0-6-0T locomotive No 41708 of 1880 simmers with her three-coach train after arriving with the 16.10 from Harman's Cross. *Andrew P. M. Wright*

'Leaving the school at the age of 14, I had to get a job and contribute to the family. I had six other brothers and sisters and my father, Ernest Weekes, had been called up into the RAF as a cook and was out in Egypt.

'My mother said there was a job going down the railway for a junior porter and I should apply for it. I came home one day and she said she'd asked for an interview for me with the stationmaster. I wasn't too pleased at the prospect of going to see the stationmaster with my mother but my father was away in the war. I suppose had he been around, then he would have gone with me.

'The appointed morning arrived and we went down the station to see Mr Nobbs in his office. He was a tall and very distinguished man — like a commander — who demanded and got respect from all the staff at Swanage.

'During the interview he looked me up and down and commented on my size — or lack of it, I think. Eventually, Mr Nobbs succumbed to my mother's persuasiveness and agreed to take me on for a three-month trial period for the princely sum of 25 shillings a week.

'The first day I started work at the station was the second or third week of September 1943. It was a cool morning when I reported to Mr Nobbs and he introduced me to the station foreman, Harold House. Mr House took me up the platform and told me to stand there and watch the men unloading mail bags off a train.'

While Albert was at Swanage, Mr Nobbs left to take up another appointment as station-master at Bournemouth during 1944 and Mr Trim came to Swanage. 'Mr Trim and Mr Nobbs were very different characters. Mr Trim came from West Moors and was very much a countryman of the old order, whereas Mr Nobbs was very upright — like a school teacher. Mr Nobbs ended his career with a management position at Waterloo station. Mr Trim's daughter later married Maurice Walton, the booking clerk, who stayed on at Swanage until the branch line was closed in 1972.'

Starting work as a junior porter at Swanage, Albert was seconded to station porter, Alec Dudley. Alec stayed on until the end of steam on Monday 5 September 1966, when three-coach 'Hampshire' DEMUs (diesel-electric multiple-units) came in to run the branch service. 'Alec had a great influence on me. With my own father away in the Middle East, Alec took his place. Alec was an extremely nice man — you couldn't pick a better chap to work with. There were two porters at Swanage then, Alec and Cecil Collins who owned a hotel just across from the station.'

For his 25 shillings a week — £1.25 in current money — Albert worked a 48-hour, six-

Centre left:
Two fondly-remembered characters from the old Swanage branch — driver Jock Hapgood and Swanage station porter/guard Alec Dudley chat together between trains in the summer of 1966, just before they both retired. It was Alec who took 14-year-old porter Albert Weekes under his wing when the youngster joined the Southern Railway from school in September 1943. 'Alec had a great influence on me — taking the place of my father who was away serving with the RAF in Egypt', remembers Albert nearly 50 years on. *Chris Phillips*

Left:
Leaning from the footplate of Victorian LSWR 'T9' class 'Greyhound' 4-4-0 No 120, Swanage Railway driver Ron Roberts chats with train guard Mark Woolley at Harman's Cross station on Sunday 9 June 1991 — before the pair leave with the 15.00 train to Swanage. Built in 1899, 'T9' No 120 is on a 10-year loan from the National Railway Museum in York. The class were known as 'Greyhounds' among footplate crews because of their swift turn of speed. *Andrew P. M. Wright*

Right:
One-time Swanage station booking clerk Dicky Dawe is seen here on the 'up' platform at Corfe Castle station in the late 1940s after taking up the post of stationmaster. Sadly, Mr Dawe was forced to retire in 1956 because of ill health and moved to Harman's Cross and a house overlooking the branch line.
Courtesy of Les Hayward

Below:
Dicky Dawe's grandson — Les Hayward — stands at Corfe Castle on Sunday 24 June 1990, as railway volunteers and staff from Tarmac Ltd relay the 'down' platform. Born in Swanage in 1943, Les lived with his mother and grandparents at Corfe station from 1949 until 1956. Watching the line wither and die, Les emigrated to Australia in 1973 but returned in 1981. Shocked to find the station rotting away, he restored the main building so it could house an electronics firm he co-founded.
Andrew P. M. Wright

day week at Swanage; starting either at 7am and finishing at 4pm on the early turn, or going in at 11.30am and finishing at 8.30pm.

'When I started there was another junior porter, Raymond 'Ginger' Broomfield, who was only in the job for a couple of months. Another new boy was London evacuee Roy White, who had moved down to a house in King's Road East in Swanage with his mother. We got very friendly despite him being over 6ft tall and me being only 4ft 11in high. He'd do one turn and I'd do the other. My half-day off was a Wednesday.

'Working Saturdays was annoying because everyone else was working a half day and enjoying themselves in the afternoon. I'd be stuck at the station so couldn't go and watch the football. At the end of my first week I walked home with my first wage packet — one pound and five shillings which was a fair bit of money in those days. The pound went to my mother, I put a shilling into a clothing club or something like that and the rest I spent.'

When Albert started at Swanage with the Southern Railway — then under the control of the Government's wartime Railway Executive Committee — the staff consisted of

30

stationmaster Mr Nobbs, station foreman Harold House — a character Albert remembers as being a 'sergeant major type, quite fierce looking with a bristling moustache and red face'. There were also the senior porters Alec Dudley and Cecil Collins, booking office staff Dicky Dawe — later stationmaster at Corfe Castle in the late 1940s after Mr Chapman — as well as Mr Cahagan, who Albert recalls as being rather aloof.

'Charlie Callen was the parcels clerk who I worked under eventually. Over in the goods shed there was Percy Massey, the checker, and Mr Beddington, the goods clerk. Fred Waterman was the goods driver then. Mr Best was the shunter and goods guard. The two signalmen at Swanage were Harry Galton and Wilf Ford. Harry's son, Arthur, was a signalman at Swanage in the 1950s and 1960s — working at Corfe Castle until the end of the line in 1972.'

The three drivers at Swanage were Bob Mitchell, Sam Boyland and Jack Spicer, whose firemen were Bill King and then Stan Brown, Stan 'Enoch' Hawkes and Jack Stockley respectively.

'After I saw off the initial trains from Swanage in the morning — the 9.30 and the 10 o'clock — I used to report to the goods yard and assist Percy Massey in unloading and loading the goods trains and itemising and labelling

Above:
A rare 1930s view of Swanage's main station building being extended by the Southern Railway. By 1937, summer traffic to the resort had become so heavy that the old 1884 station could not cope and in November 1937, plans were drawn up to more than double capacity. This picture was taken looking towards the buffer stops from the forecourt on the sunny morning of Sunday 22 May 1938. To the left, the old 1884 lavatories wait to be knocked down.
Courtesy of Les Hayward

Left:
A view of the station platform looking towards Corfe Castle on Sunday 22 May 1938, with the new extension and steelwork for the extended canopy fast taking shape. From left to right are the stationmaster's office, the gentlemen's and ladies' lavatories, the waiting room and bookstall. Italian craftsmen were imported to do the terrazzo tiling work in the new lavatories.
Courtesy of Les Hayward

parcels and the like. I still remember the orange luggage and parcel labels for the Somerset & Dorset line.

'Finishing in the goods shed, I'd go back on to the platform again when the porters would collect the signal lamps from around the station and we'd sit down, clean them and then fill them up again with paraffin. In the afternoon we'd clean the spare carriages before the workers' train came in.

'Later on, Mr Nobbs found out that there was pressure building up in the parcels office, so I was transferred to work with Charlie Callen. That meant an increase in pay to two pounds and ten shillings a week, which was great. I worked in the parcels office for about two years.

'Charlie was a real character. He came from Southampton and I think he used to play in pantomimes before the war. I remember on VE-Day in May 1945 — when everybody was very relaxed and just elated the war was over — that he came into work dressed up as a French sailor, complete with make-up on his face. He had found a barrel organ from somewhere and pushed it around the town playing it.'

But, a Swanage station employee who Albert remembers with most fondness is Alec Dudley — the station porter and guard who stayed at Swanage until the autumn of 1966. 'I got on really well with Alec,' Albert recalls. 'Originally a Londoner, he jumped ship as a youngster and got to Canada where he spent some time working. He really used to put on the style a bit. In fact, I can remember him showing me some faded snapshots of him dressed as a cowboy which was quite something because they were our heroes in those days.

'The Yanks were very impressed with Alec after he showed them the pictures of himself as a cowboy. In fact, he became friendly with two GIs who used to regularly come down to the station with their truck to collect stuff off the train. They used to bring him chewing gum and cigarettes and sit and talk with him. We'd have a laugh and a joke and then they'd be off.

'The station at Swanage seemed to be a place where lonely people used to come during the war — especially the Americans. I suppose they felt that sometime they'd be getting on that train themselves and going home.'

Nearly half a century after it happened, Albert Weekes can still clearly recall the day he saw the first American GIs arrive in Swanage by train — the first of three troop trains to arrive in the seaside town.

'Alec Dudley told me the night before to come in an hour early at 6am instead of 7am because there was a special train coming down. He wouldn't say any more — careless talk, you know. Anyway, I turned up for work the following morning. It was cold and still dark with snow and ice on the platform. I sprinkled sand on the platform and put the trolleys out ready to take the Americans' equipment.

'Then the train came in — absolutely crammed full of GIs with their kitbags and carbine rifles. The train was so long that it stretched from the stopblocks beyond the platform to the Northbrook road bridge. Then the doors opened and they swarmed out on to the platform. I helped them get out with their heavy back packs on and their rifles. The running boards of the carriages were covered with ice so they needed assistance.

'I can remember the first American I helped off the train. I was struck by how dark and tanned his face was. I later found out he had returned from the landings in Sicily and North Africa. He said "Hi kid," and I replied, "Watch your step, fella," as I helped him off. He thanked me and then I went on down the platform helping others.

'Their equipment on the end of the train such as jeeps and other vehicles were off-loaded via the cattle dock in the yard and a wooden sleeper dock built off the goods shed road — near the old lamp hut by the bay track. I often used to clean the lamps in there and then scive off by playing cards or having a snooze between trains.

'To us youngsters, the Americans seem to step straight out of Hollywood and the Wild West — speaking just like the stars and chewing gum to boot. After they got off the train, it was chaos for 20 minutes as the tired and travel-weary troops assembled on the platform. They then marched off to their new billets in local hotels and us porters got on board the train to clean it out and check that nothing had been left behind.

'I remember the Yanks lost a typewriter on the train and there was hell to pay. They were screaming and shouting about it as they tried to find it. We searched through the train three or four times and eventually found it in some nook and cranny but the Americans had marched off. One of us — Alec Dudley, Roy White or me — found a carbine rifle on one of the luggage racks.

'We contacted the American authorities in town but they didn't seem to care about claiming it. We kept it in the lost property section of the booking office at Swanage for weeks before we persuaded the US Army to come down and collect it. We were surprised they seemed more concerned about a typewriter rather than the rifle.'

Another spin-off from the troop trains for the

Left:
The late Phyllis Cook, manageress of the W. H. Smith bookstalls at Wareham and Swanage stations, received national publicity in October 1943, for sacrificing a valued gold wristwatch to encourage local people to buy National Savings Certificates and help the war effort. 'It was a great wrench to part with it, but I thought maybe it would be the means of bringing the lads home a little sooner,' she said proudly at the time.
Courtesy of Bryan Green

N.S.News

October, 1943   Issued by the W.H.S. National Savings Association   No. 14

GAVE VALUED KEEPSAKE TO ENCOURAGE SAVING

A gold wrist watch, of great sentimental value to the owner, was the means of raising £35.5.0 for the Nation during the "Wings for Victory" Week at Swanage recently.

The donor of the watch was Mrs. P. M. Cook, temporary manageress of Swanage stall, and to her goes credit for the idea that enabled the Southern Railway savings group to over-shoot its target despite strong competition.

"The station master obtained a bomb which was placed in the booking hall," Mrs. Cook told *N.S. News.* "He asked me if I would co-operate in the selling of stamps. Of course I agreed, but somehow I couldn't see us reaching the £25 target, because there were so many other interests in the town, and two more bombs anyway. I could see our poor little bomb being passed by the folk hurrying to and from the

trains! So I suggested running a competition. I had a tiny gold wrist watch of great sentimental value to me, and I offered it as a prize to attract the people.

———— *See Page Two*

"Believe me, it was a great wrench to part with it, but I thought maybe it would be the means of bringing the lads home a little sooner." Mrs. Cook, of Swanage stall, who sacrificed her gold wrist watch so that others would give to the Nation.

★ ————————— ★
Total to August 28
W. H. S. sales of National Savings Certificates reached £267,906 . 15 . 0 on August 28, 1943.
★ ————————— ★

Bristol Tops £2400 in One-Week Drive

The slogan "Double figures in 1943" is showing results! We have received the good news that Bristol House has scored a "double" — and the nation is better off by £2,461 10s. 0d.

To reach this figure Bristol House had to increase the average weekly takings by more than 300 times.

"Our usual weekly takings are £8 1s. 0d. per week," writes Mr. H. L. Howarth, "and our target was £1,000. We purchased £2,525 worth of certificates, of

which £2,461 10s. 0d. were sold during the week, and the balance sold later."

Chief credit for the outstanding success of W. H. Smith's part in Bristol's "Wings for Victory" Week goes to two ladies—Miss M. Dawe, Bristol House accountant, and Mrs. F. M. Wills, senior counting-house clerk.

"They certainly did put in some hard work," Mr. Howarth adds—and so say all of us!

———— *See Page Three*

railway staff were the rations that were left on board by the tired American troops when they reached Swanage.

'The GIs brought with them the famous K-Rations, of course. They really were marvellous and contained food we'd never seen and certainly couldn't get hold of because of rationing. Our troops would perhaps be given sandwiches and an orange on their trains but the Yanks had K-Rations in a special waxed cardboard box with chocolate, biscuits and a five-pack of cigarettes — Camels, Lucky Strike or Chesterfields. They really did contain everything, even a small tin of ham and eggs as well as cans of cheese, potted meat, orange and lemon powder.

'There was also chewing gum, powdered coffee, sugar and sweets rather like our polo mints but fruit flavoured. As we were cleaning out the train, we'd search through the boxes left by the troops to see if there was any food left. Because the platform staff were spare, we'd have first pickings — the poor goods checkers and signalmen couldn't leave their posts. Parcels clerk Charlie Callen organised us platform staff and persuaded us to go through the long train methodically and collect what we could for a general pool. We came off best in the end — the men had the cigarettes and we had the chewing gum, the thick slab chocolate and the biscuits.

'We didn't know it at the time but the GIs were billeted in Swanage while they trained

Albert Weekes sits at the second ticket window of Swanage station's booking office in June 1991, from where he issued hundreds of train tickets to eager American GIs off to Bournemouth and London on leave in 1943 and 1944. With Albert are modern-day GIs Simon and Andrew Spenceley and Steve Bennett of the Military Vehicle Conservation Group's Dorset branch.
Andrew P. M. Wright

for the D-Day Allied landings in Normandy the following summer. Tragically, many of the men that came to Swanage that winter were not to come back.

'The Americans were mostly jolly and generous people who especially liked youngsters — I suppose it reminded them of their families back home. But, I did notice that they managed to keep hold of their money. They used to play dice and cards on the platform while they were waiting for the train — throwing their notes on the ground.

'After watching this a few times, Roy White and I thought up a ruse to try and get some of the money. We'd shout that the train had arrived and that they should hurry to catch it. Our hope was that they'd panic and leave a few bob on the ground — but they never did. They were pretty sharp.

'They were generous and certainly would give you something if you asked. They were always giving chocolate, sweets and gum to local children and cigarettes to the adults. They were things that were heavily rationed so to see them so freely available — and in such quantities — was something. A couple of my friends became friendly with the Americans and visited them in their billets. They used to get tins of fruit and all sorts of things.

'I remember two GIs who became very friendly with Alec Dudley and came down for a chat almost every day. They always used to carry chewing gum and bring a carton of Raleigh cigarettes for Alec. Apparently, one of the GI's well-meaning aunts used to regularly send him packets from the States with other goodies. They couldn't stand the brand but didn't have the heart to tell his relation, so the soldier used to pass them on to Alec who was more than pleased.

'One of the Americans used to ride an odd-looking British bicycle — a rarity during the war. I'll always remember the sight of this GI riding along the platform on this upright Victorian bicycle. When he left for D-Day, he sold it to Alec, who used to ride it to work for years afterwards.

'Another infantryman used to come and sit on the station in the evening instead of going out boozing with his friends. He used to talk a lot about home. When I asked him why he didn't join his mates, he said he thought there were going to be some good opportunities after the war ended and he got home — and he wasn't going to drink away his money. "I'm gonna save my money, kid," he'd say.'

The late Mrs Phyllis Cook managed the railway bookstalls at Swanage and Wareham stations throughout the war while her husband Harold was serving in the Far East with the RAF. She used to give Albert Weekes cups of Nescafe coffee. Mrs Cook also remembered the American troops vividly. The young men from across the Atlantic were regular customers at her W. H. Smith kiosk on the platform and made a lasting impression.

One memory of the young strange-sounding men from thousands of miles away was especially strong and poignant — and was to stay with her right up until her death in 1991, at the age of 84. 'It was a very clear and frosty early morning in Swanage just before Christmas 1943 — about 5am. The sky was clear and brilliant with stars,' she remembered. 'Several companies of American soldiers had gathered on the station platform, waiting for their train to come in.

'Suddenly, one young man looked up at the sky and, seeing the stars, started to sing *Silent Night, Holy Night*. A second soldier picked it up, then a third and a fourth until all the GIs were singing the lovely carol so very reverently and sincerely — and in perfect harmony.

'I've never heard anything quite so beautiful in my whole life. I just sat in my blacked-out station bookstall and sobbed my heart out. I can never hear *Silent Night* now without remembering those American lads on the platform — bound for who knows where.'

In October 1943, the respected and well-liked manageress of Swanage station's bookstall received national publicity throughout Britain for sacrificing a gold wristwatch of great sentimental value to boost the public's acquisition of the Government's National Savings Certificates — and boost the war effort. The donation of the watch enabled the Southern Railway savings group to raise the grand total of £35 5s; overshooting the branch line's target, despite tough competition.

Mrs Cook told the W. H. Smith National Savings Association's newsletter in 1943:

'Believe me, it was a great wrench to part with it, but I thought maybe it would be the means of bringing the lads home a little sooner.' She added: 'The stationmaster obtained a bomb which was placed in the booking hall at Swanage. He asked me if I'd co-operate in the selling of stamps. Of course, I agreed but somehow I couldn't see us reaching the £25 target because there were so many other interests in the town.

'I could see our poor little bomb being passed by the folk hurrying to and from the trains! So, I suggested running a competition. I had a tiny gold wristwatch of great sentimental value to me, and I offered it as a prize to attract the people.

'We set to it and sold tickets at one shilling each. RAF personnel billeted locally were marvellous in helping to sell them, and we were receiving telephone calls from everywhere for them. When we found that "trade" was so good we decided to offer a Savings Certificate as second prize and saving stamps as other prizes.'

Seeing Allied Commander General Dwight D. Eisenhower at the start of his two-day visit to Swanage on Friday 11 February 1944, also made a vivid impression on 15-year-old Albert Weekes.

'Eisenhower, General Montgomery, King George VI and Prime Minister Winston Churchill came down to Swanage to review the troops and watch rehearsals at Studland for the D-Day landings in Normandy. No-one knew they were going to arrive at the station except the top brass. Roy White was on the early turn at Swanage on the day that the three special trains arrived. The King's train had evidently been kept at Corfe Castle or Furzebrook sidings before coming down to Swanage station.

'Later, when I came on duty I did get to see General Eisenhower. The King's train was already at Swanage when the American Commander's came into the main platform and Eisenhower got off. His train was different to Montgomery's with big round-topped carriages — rather like Pullmans — in a brown and maroon colour. Montgomery's train, known as "the Rapier", was put in the yard where the car park now is. It was different, much more sober and more old-fashioned with brass handrails at the doors.

'Alec Dudley and I were on the late turn that day and he asked me if I wanted to go out

Below left:
As Allied forces pushed through Normandy heading for Paris in July 1944, Swanage station held a fund-raising 'Salute The Soldier' week from Saturday 1 July to Saturday 8 July 1944. The aim was to encourage local people to buy more war savings and help the war effort. From left to right: track ganger Edwin Bird, driver Charlie Boyland, signalman Wilf Ford, W. H. Smith bookstall manageress Phyllis Cook, Colonel Seldon from Salisbury, another Army officer and Dorchester-based cleaner Stan Brown by the 2lb gun. Stan was to move to Swanage as a fireman in September 1944.
William Powell, courtesy of Edwin Bird

Bottom left:
Station porter Albert Weekes is reunited with ex-branch fireman Stan Brown at Swanage on Saturday 8 June 1991, for the first time since 1947 when Albert was drafted into the Army and National Service. Becoming a fireman at Swanage in September 1944, Stan moved to Bournemouth MPD in 1947. Here, Stan is seen in the same place as the previous picture but the 2lb gun he was minding during the 'Salute The Soldier' week in July 1944, has long gone.
Andrew P. M. Wright

and see General Eisenhower go by. It was a nice evening. We saw the general with his military aides walk down the platform. We stood to attention, nodded and said good evening and he replied and smiled. He walked through the booking office and into a waiting car — waving and smiling to the small crowd — before being driven through the town.

'We were able to get on board the train and see his private cinema on board where they were running cartoons. It was marvellous to have movies on a train. We then went across into the yard and saw Monty's train and the mobile office in which he worked. It seemed more open than Eisenhower's train which appeared very dark. Security I suppose.

'It was a nice evening so I asked Alec if I could go for a walk down to the seafront and watch the rehearsals. I sat up on the recreation ground and watched the aircraft fly over Ballard Down before disappearing out of sight dropping their bombs at Studland.'

Albert remembers the panic caused amongst staff at Swanage the first weekend that the GIs were given weekend passes or leave — and made a rush for the train.

'There used to be a special return ticket for servicemen wanting to get from Swanage to London. It cost £1/–/3 and very popular it was, too. At the weekends when they were given passes, the Americans headed straight away for Bournemouth and London and the only way they could get there was by train. The first Saturday they were given passes we were completely unaware of the volume of soldiers that would descend on the station to

catch the 1.35pm fast train to London that used to get into Waterloo around 5pm.

'GIs started drifting on to the platform from about 12 noon. We thought nothing of it. To our surprise, by 12.30pm the platform was completely crammed with soldiers waiting for the train. It was incredible, we'd never seen anything like it before. We didn't open the ticket office at Swanage until about 20 minutes before the train would leave but there was no way we could sell that many tickets to the Yanks in that time.

'I can remember a surprised Alec Dudley running into the booking office and telling clerk Dicky Dawe he'd better open up the window and sell some tickets pretty sharpish. Dicky opened up the window and couldn't believe what he saw — the booking hall crammed full of soldiers, a jolly bunch, all wanting to buy tickets.

'We started selling tickets as fast as we could at 12.45pm but there was no way we could get them all sold in time for the train leaving at 1.35pm. When the departure time came and we were still frantically selling tickets, there was some strong talk from the guard of the London train. Of course, the train went out late that afternoon — much to the anger of the crew and the guard who was responsible for any late running.

'Anyway, an answer to the problem was quickly thought out by booking clerks Dicky Dawe and Mr Callen. The following week we pre-stamped a huge pile of servicemen's concessionary tickets for the coming Saturday. On the day, the second ticket window — normally unused and virtually rusted up — was pressed into action. The Americans were asked to have the right money ready and I was sat there to dish out the tickets so the GIs could catch their train — and it could leave on time. After that, we had no more problems.'

There were three trains a day from Swanage to Holton Heath for the war workers making shell explosives for the Admiralty at the factory there. They covered the shifts that started at 10pm, 6am and 2pm. Because most of the workers were women doing war work, since most men of working age had been called up and gone off to war, the trains were known to the Americans as the 'glamour puffers'.

'Although the Americans were only in Swanage for six months or so, seen through the eyes of a youngster like me it seemed like a long time because there was so much going on. Many local girls married Americans — and those that returned from Normandy alive took their new wives over to the United States to live.

Right:
Swanage station in 1943 or 1944? No, a scene that stirred many bitter-sweet memories during a special 1940s weekend in September 1990. Veteran ex-BR driver Stan Symes chats with 'Yanks' John Ilott and Shelagh Spink of the Military Vehicle Conservation Group's Dorset branch from the footplate of Great Eastern Railway 'N7' class 0-6-2T locomotive No 69621. Built in 1924, the restored N7 was on loan to the Swanage Railway during 1990 from the East Anglian Railway Museum.
Andrew P. M. Wright

'When the GIs left Swanage it was as though the world stopped turning — it was hectic while they were in the town and then all the activity suddenly stopped. I was amazed how the authorities kept the D-Day beach landings so secret. I can remember chatting to Americans as they waterproofed their jeeps and other vehicles near the station with a curious green gunge that looked like Plasticine. We knew something was on from all the preparations but not where or when.'

The day the Americans left Swanage for further D-Day preparations was a warm day in April 1944. 'It was a nice sunny day as I recall,' Albert remembers. 'The first Yanks started arriving at the station just after 9am and waited in the goods yard by the old cattle dock and on the station forecourt with their kit. They talked, smoked and chatted as they lay on their kitbags. Because it was quite a warm day, someone went round giving out water as they waited for the train to come in.

Above left:
Swanage station's gas-lit parcels office in the summer of 1966 complete with the large Pooley weighing scales in the middle of the lofty room. Porter Bill 'Taffy' Hazell is to the far left with porter/shunter Tom Tetley to his right. In the left-hand corner of the office is the door to the booking office. Porter/shunter George Symes is sat working to the right, with the enquiry window behind him. *Chris Phillips*

Left:
In June 1991, Albert Weekes stands where he spent five years working as a porter, for the first time since 1947. The old parcels office has now become the Swanage Railway's busy shop, modern electric strip lights replacing the old gas lights. In 1972, the station was boarded up prior to sale and probable demolition — the old parcels office left to gather dust. Railway volunteers managed to lease the decaying station buildings in 1976 after a four-year battle with the local council.
Andrew P. M. Wright

SOUTHERN RAILWAY.
(2/27) TO
CORFE CASTLE
Stock 787

A few girls and other local people turned up to say goodbye to their new-found friends and Alec's two friends came in to say farewell, too.

'In the end, the train finally came in and they boarded it but were kept waiting for quite a long time for some reason. I can remember walking along the platform and along the track to the signalbox as the troops leaned out of the train windows. They were cheerful and giving the thumbs up sign to me. I smiled and returned the gesture and then the long train finally left sometime between 1.30 and 2pm. I always wondered what happened to them on D-Day and if they survived.'

After the long troop train had left, the good-humoured chatter and wisecracking had gone. Instead, there was silence — with only a few discarded cigarette packets and chewing gum wrappers left on the platform to show that the American infantrymen had ever been there. Once the war came to an end, the Swanage branch line returned to its normal life as a seaside station. Albert stayed at Swanage until June 1947, when he reached his 18th birthday and was called up for his National Service in the Royal Artillery. 'I was sad on my last day because the station staff were like a family to me. I was still quite shy and didn't like any kind of fuss, although I'd really grown up between 1943 and 1947. The staff had a whip-round for me and I can remember going round the station saying goodbye to everybody.'

After coming out of the Army in 1949, Albert returned to the family home in Swanage but felt that he wanted to get more out of life — to see places outside of his home town. After a career installing telephones around the country, Albert returned to Purbeck and a new home in Wareham in the mid-1960s.

'I was annoyed the way British Rail ran down the Swanage line and eventually closed it. It dismayed a lot of the old staff — they all felt deeply betrayed. I can recall coming to Swanage on holiday with my wife and our young family. We were travelling by bus from Corfe when I noticed Dicky Dawe on board. I said "hello" to him and had a quick chat as we got off the bus. I thought I'd see him again and that he'd be around for ever. The next thing I knew he had died of a heart attack,' recalls Albert thoughtfully.

'Dicky was a jolly chap — always whistling — with a jaunty sort of walk and a moustache. He used to roll his own cigarettes and smoke medium shag tobacco that I used to fetch for him from the tobacconists in Institute Road, Swanage. Supplies of tobacco — like most things — were short during the war but we knew when new stocks came into town because they'd come in by train and I'd have to deliver the parcel. That way, Dicky always got his supplies before they sold out.

'I still occasionally go down to Swanage station and have a wander round with my wife. It hasn't changed much — apart from the bus company and taxi firm using half the station. It's strange to go into what's now the railway shop but was then the parcels office where I worked with old Charlie Callen. Some of the old enamel signs are up under the station canopy and it looks as though the railway has never been away.'

Albert still clearly recalls D-Day, 6 June 1944, after the Americans who had made such an impact on Swanage were fighting for their lives on the other side of the Channel — and sustaining horrific casualties in a bid to cling on to Normandy and a vital piece of Fortress Europe. 'I started work at 6.30am instead of 7am that Tuesday morning because I'd often have a cup of tea with Alec. It was very quiet. We were on the platform when two American Typhoon aircraft flew over the town, headed for France. I turned to Alec, saying that I sensed there was something different about the morning but I didn't know what.'

At lunchtime that day, the staff of Swanage station clustered round Dicky Dawe's old radio in the booking office and heard the momentous news that the Allies had landed on the northern coast of France.

However, it was bitter-sweet news because the young men of the First Division that Albert and his colleagues at Swanage had laughed and joked with just a few weeks before were now being ruthlessly cut down by enemy fire on the beaches — like ripe summer corn before the harvester's scythe. At the end of the 'longest day' on Omaha beach that June, over a thousand American GIs had been slaughtered and thousands more horrifically injured — an experience that would be burnt on the memories of survivors for the rest of their lives.

The American GIs' Tale

'The Swanage railroad was a vital link to happy times with new-found friends. It took us away from the harshness of training for war and was a friendly little line. I still recall it and remember the kind people I met there with affection.'

Bill Lee, Ex-Second World War American GI

'Gees, it sure ain't changed,' comes the excited exclamation, the 70-year-old American's eyes lighting up as he walks on to Swanage station platform with a group of other 'veterans'. He tells his equally excited wife what it was like on the same spot nearly half a century before during World War 2. Back in 1944, he had more spring in his step, despite carrying a heavy back-pack and a carbine rifle.

The American veteran was little more than a teenager then — thrown into a new, strange country and preparing to fight for his life in the largest and most daring maritime invasion in history; just 70 miles across the English Channel from Swanage.

Nearly 50 years later, the one-time soldiers of the First Division's 26th Infantry Regiment — now retired and almost all grandfathers — still remember their time in Swanage and the importance of its railway station to them during their brief but memorable stay in the town back in 1943 and 1944.

Ex-GI Jack Gray — now living in Colorado, but then a Platoon Sergeant — remembers the branch line clearly, despite being over five thousand miles away and 47 years later.

'Every time the train pulled out of the station it was crowded and with standing room only. Unless you got there early and got on the train as soon as it came in, you'd never get a compartment. If you did, you could pull down the blind so you and your lady friend had some privacy. But, if you didn't, you just had to stand out in the corridor for the journey.

'The staff at Swanage were always polite and pleasant despite having to fight their way through the crowd of GIs to check tickets. I can't say enough about the railway staff — they were always there to give a helping hand and answer questions, and sort out our money for us. We all certainly owe a big thank you to them.

'Coming back to Swanage after a weekend pass was always the worst. Nearly every GI had had more than his fair share of dark and light beer so instead of standing, we'd lay down on the floor of the corridor — any place we could just curl up. But, the railway staff made sure we always got off at the right stop.

'We made several trips to Bournemouth and London. On a trip back to see Swanage in 1989 with some of the fellows, it was great to see the railway station again. I could see myself getting on the train with all the other GIs, even though it was nearly 50 years before.'

Fellow GI, Alden Peckham, from Freeport, Maine — as Private First Class in 1944 — recalls: 'I used to take the railroad from Swanage to Bournemouth every two weeks or so. One thing we thought unusual and which were a novelty and fascinated us were the compartments because we didn't have them on American railroads. We were used to having open coaches. I also remember that the train was always stopping and starting on its way from Swanage to Bournemouth. It was always easy to have a conversation with fellow passengers on the train — and being a foreigner, they made for a good feeling and lasting memories.'

Ex-First Division infantryman Jim Foore from Tonawanda, New York, and his buddies came up with a novel system of beating the crowds and remembering exactly where they had left their seats on the train.

'One time, I used WAAF lipstick to mark the carriage we were to get back on. That lipstick certainly saved the day. I always remember my first ride on the train from Swanage in late 1943 because I visited Corfe Castle. What a beautiful place that was. I'll always remember that day — getting off the train and seeing the ruins for the first time. It was quite a thrill to see it again 45 years later.

'With their long corridors and small compartments, the carriages were different at Swanage from the ones we were used to back

home, where we had open cars with seats facing each other. I can remember asking the railway staff to wake me and the other fellows up when we reached Swanage. The staff were great — helping us to find our way in a strange country,' remembers the one-time sergeant.

Ex-GI Jon Babyak, from Mc Keesport in Pennsylvania, was staying with his fellow infantrymen in the cramped confines of one of Swanage's requisitioned hotels, the Durlston Court — and lucky enough to be just across the road from an ATS billet. But, he remembers the Swanage branch line for a more personal reason.

'We rode the railroad from Swanage almost every weekend because I had a girlfriend who lived in Bournemouth but was a Wren stationed in Southampton. For some reason, I remember Wareham and Kingston.

'The train always seemed odd to us Americans because the little engine was always on the wrong end of the train — pushing instead of pulling. And sometimes we saw it wedged between two lots of coaches. We just didn't have that back in the States,' recalls the ex-GI, a Private in 1943.

'The railroad with its small compartments and seats facing each other was good because you got to meet a lot of people — and as Americans in a strange country, we liked to talk and were inquisitive. I met a lot of nice people that way. Although the trains ran on time from Swanage, I can remember them keeping up time and speeding when they had to.

'Many a time we'd squeeze 10 or 12 fellows into one compartment. Americans could be a bit unruly at times — especially when we'd had a bit too much of the half and half and Scotch, but it was fun. I used to like leaning out of the window and watch the English countryside pass by. I can remember the odd leather straps for pulling down the window.'

Left:
Thirty years later, the lineside undergrowth has increased and a plantation of pine trees sprouted behind the railway embankment. On the morning of Tuesday 17 July 1991, BR Class 47 diesel-electric locomotive No 47157 rattles down the 1 in 78 gradient — heading for Worgret Junction with the twice-weekly ball clay train from ECC Ball Clays' works at Furzebrook. The Swanage branch connected with Victorian narrow gauge tramways, serving clay pits around Furzebrook and Creech, owned by Pike Brothers Fayle & Co until 1957. *Andrew P. M. Wright*

Centre left:
With just days to live, the Swanage branch train service is used by two villagers from Corfe Castle. A three-coach 'Hampshire' DEMU, No 1105, whines into Corfe station's 'down' platform from Wareham with a midday train to Swanage on a bright but chilly winter's day in December 1971. During the branch's final years, Corfe station displayed a depressingly heavy air of neglect. Just seven months after this picture was taken, the railway was gone completely. *Mike Esau*

Bottom left:
This is what faced the volunteers of the Swanage Railway Project when they reached Corfe Castle. Sixteen years after the previous picture, Corfe station's 'down' platform is completely choked with undergrowth on Saturday 4 July 1987 — the ruins of the medieval castle only just visible behind the trees. The enamel station sign is long gone with packed steam trains arriving from Wareham, Bournemouth, Southampton and London just a faded memory. *Andrew P. M. Wright*

Right:
Four years later, determined Swanage Railway volunteers had cleared the platforms and trackbed at Corfe station of all weeds and undergrowth. Here on Sunday 24 June 1990, volunteers from Tarmac Quarry Products and Tarmac Roadstone assist with clearing the 'down' platform prior to the relaying of a new surface.
Andrew P. M. Wright

Centre right:
Trains to the hustle and bustle of London from Corfe Castle and Swanage were a vital link with normality for the American GIs training for war in the Isle of Purbeck. On a warm summer afternoon, streamlined 'West Country' class Bulleid Pacific No 34042 *Dorchester* speeds round the curve past Norden Heath — between Corfe Castle and Furzebrook — with the 10-coach 13.23 Swanage to Waterloo through train on Saturday 23 August 1958.
Sid C. Nash

Bottom right:
Was this really a railway just 19 years before? Looking towards Corfe Castle, the weed and tree-choked trackbed past Norden Heath that No 34042 *Dorchester* ran over on a hot summer afternoon in 1958 lies silent on Sunday 21 July 1991. Lying dormant for six months after the last BR train ran, the track through here was torn up for scrap during the middle of August 1972.
Andrew P. M. Wright

For Richard Biehl of the 26th Infantry of the 'Big Red One', now retired in the small town of Temple, Pennsylvania, one morning at Swanage station in Christmas 1943 was a special occasion — and one he still recalls, nearly 50 years later.

'I always remember the train station at Swanage because I boarded the train there early one morning. It was 22 December 1943, and the start of my leave — seven glorious days up in London. Everyone was most friendly and cordial and riding a train in England was a very new experience for me — but all went well. The chug-chug-chug of the steam engine and its shrill whistle will always stay with me,' he adds thoughtfully.

For Danny D'Allessandro from the Brooklyn district of New York, it was the opportunity to meet ordinary Dorset people that makes the Swanage branch railway memorable.

'I remember having a lot of fun on the train. Everyone was very friendly to us. We'd sing songs, down a few beers and feel quite good by the time we reached our destination. Whenever I'm on a train in the States, I always talk about my trips by train up and down the line between Wareham and Swanage.

'As strangers in a new country, we enjoyed the closeness of the passengers, their pleasant faces and their warmth. The small compartments got you talking to people — and, of course, if there was a pretty girl with us, we'd try to ask her out. We didn't often succeed but it was fun trying.

'But, if we missed the last train from Wareham down to Swanage we'd have to hitch-hike back to camp, causing us to miss reveille and meaning that we'd get lumbered with kitchen duty as a punishment.

'When I saw Swanage and the railroad again in 1989, I became quite choked. I'll never forget the experience and the people I met on the railroad back then.'

Another ex-GI, Warren Coffmann — then a Private — from Winter Springs in Florida, remembers the day when he first saw Swanage from the carriage window of the branch train one morning in November 1943.

'We had travelled down from a replacement depot in Birmingham. Before we left Swanage in April 1944, I and my fellow GIs always used the train to go to Bournemouth or London on weekend passes. Without the train being there we couldn't have done that because we didn't have any other transport available.

'It was unusual to have the platform level with the train because back home we were used to having steps at each end of the car — and a conductor who'd bring out a pair of steps when the train came into a station.

'One thing that surprised me when I first went to the station was the fact that you had to buy a platform ticket to meet someone off the train. Back home as kids we used to go down to the local train depot, walk on the platform without paying and watch the trains arriving, just to see who got off.'

For a homesick 23-year-old GI from Mount Vernon — a small town in central Illinois — the branch line to Swanage was an unexpected and bitter-sweet reminder of home. An ex-postmaster of Mount Vernon, Bill Lee is now retired and recalls those wartime days with surprising affection.

'The Swanage railroad reminded me of a small line called the Wabash, Chester & Western Railway Company we had back home in Jefferson County, Illinois. We used to call it the "Wait, Charlie and Walk" railroad because of its unhurried pace. It may have been the same size as the Swanage railroad but that was where the similarity ended because the line from Wareham was effective, clean and ran to time. Without it we couldn't have got out of Swanage on our weekend passes.

'Although it drew a great deal of ridicule from the GIs at first, because it was small and looked quaint, they soon realised the Swanage railroad was a vital link to happy times with newly-found girlfriends in Wareham, Poole and Bournemouth. It took us away from the harshness of training for war during those times and was a friendly little line,' remembers the wartime Private.

Although across the Atlantic, Bill Lee still recalls with affection the people of Swanage and its branch railway who offered the hand of friendship to strange young men from another land back in 1943 and 1944.

'The people of the Purbecks were an important part of our lives for those seven months, and we needed that. We were brash, different, full of bravado but they took us in as part of their families — and for that we will always be grateful and never forget.

'Our brash, happy, outgoing exteriors were just veneers — a cover because we didn't want to get hurt at a time when close, personal and intimate friends were being killed — there one minute, gone out of our lives the next.

'The railroad through Purbeck was a valuable link with our new home-from-home down in Swanage. Although nearly fifty years later and 4,000 miles away, I still clearly remember it and the kind people I met then.'

43

The Wartime Fireman's Tale

'There we were – walking along the seafront when we were amazed to see General Montgomery walking towards us. He was calmly throwing his maroon beret into the air and catching it. I just couldn't believe it.'

Doug Scott

The grimy face of a portly engine driver squints up at the bright sky one sunny late afternoon in 1941 as he sits on the footplate of his squat tank engine — his young fireman below busy coupling up the train.

Suddenly, the growl of four Messerschmitt Me109 fighters drown the reassuring sound of the two dirty steam locomotives as they simmer patiently at Swanage's main platform — ready to haul the afternoon school train to Corfe Castle and Wareham. The German aircraft race low over the rooftops of the closely packed houses on the other side of the station yard — tiny specks of black that suddenly became frighteningly discernible shapes.

'Here Doug, see those aircraft?' points out Hamworthy driver Wilf Selby hesitantly. He is about to continue when an awful realisation sweeps over him.

About to couple the vacuum brake pipe to the second steam locomotive, the next thing 20-year-old Bournemouth fireman Doug Scott feels is 12 stone of driver Selby throwing himself down on the young man. A split second later, there is a series of explosions. The ground shakes. There is a deafening crashing sound as glass in the long station canopy shatters into thousands of lethal, razor-sharp shards. Debris and choking dust fly everywhere, settling like a fine coat of icing sugar.

Then, there is an awful silence — apart from the hissing of steam from the two locomotives. Some of the children on the train begin to cry and there are shouts from the 'M7's footplate crew. Fireman Scott and driver Selby crawl from under their tank locomotive, dust themselves down and look around in disbelief.

Now a Bournemouth pensioner but still working, Doug Scott has good reason to remember the old Swanage branch line because that is where he could have easily been killed half a century ago. That frightening air raid on Wednesday 14 May 1941, was one of the worst the small seaside resort of Swanage ever experienced, with several peo-

ple killed and many commercial properties and private houses flattened or severely damaged.

'I still remember that day clearly as though it was just yesterday,' says Doug now sitting in the comfort of his armchair 50 years later. 'We were in a hurry to get away and the guard was, too. After checking the children were uninjured we made a rapid departure from the station bound for Corfe Castle.'

However, as the double-headed train gathered speed past the houses of King's Road, along the long straight to Victoria Avenue and out past the gasworks siding to Herston — the site of a halt 38 years later — the crews

Right:
Doug Scott and Stan Symes are reunited at Swanage on Sunday 23 September 1990 — 50 years after they last worked together for the Southern Railway. Not knowing they both lived in the same road of a Bournemouth suburb, Doug and Stan both joined the Southern Railway on Monday 28 August 1939 — just a week before the outbreak of World War 2. *Andrew P. M. Wright*

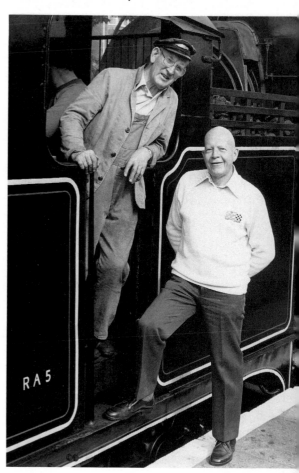

44

of both engines were unaware their problems were not over. 'What we didn't know was that I'd forgotten to connect the vacuum pipe working the brakes on the "M7" behind us and the carriages. The only brakes working were on our tank engine,' adds Doug with a smile. 'Anyway, we were able to stop the train at Corfe Castle using our handbrake. I got off and connected the pipe as the driver told the station staff what had just happened back at Swanage.'

Although he was only on the railways for six years, and then only forced out of the industry through ill-health, the Swanage branch line has a special place in Doug Scott's heart.

Born in the Winton suburb of Bournemouth, Doug was the son of a Poole joiner. By chance, he joined the Southern Railway on the same day as future Swanage branch and main line driver Stan Symes — who lived in the same road as Doug — on

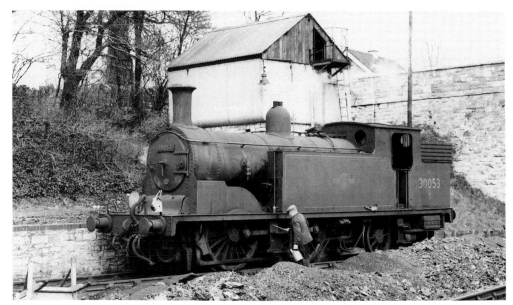

Above left:
Senior Swanage driver Jack Spicer oils up Victorian 'M7' 0-4-4T No 30053 at the terminus' coaling stage and water tower between trains on Friday 10 April 1964. The last 'M7' was to run on the branch less than four weeks later. Water to the LSWR water tank — manufactured by Brown & Bobby Engineers of London — was supplied from a well thanks to a pump operated by the steam locomotive's pressure. Built in 1905, No 30053 was withdrawn from regular traffic in May 1964, stored at Eastleigh before being sold to an American millionaire in 1967. *David Esau*

Left:
Twenty years after leaving Liverpool Docks for the USA and the Steamtown Museum, 'M7' 0-4-4T No 30053 is back at Swanage station and its coaling dock on the evening of Friday 22 May 1987. The 'M7' is seen with 1880-built Midland '1F' 0-6-0T No 41708, then on loan from the Midland Railway Centre in Derbyshire but now permanently based at Swanage. 'M7' No 30053 had made a triumphant return to the Isle of Purbeck from the USA the previous month — exactly 23 years since she steamed out of Swanage for the last time in BR service. *Andrew P. M. Wright*

miles and work on something like 97 different forms of traction, including steam, diesel and electric.

At the end of his first week, Doug walked up the ramp from the soot-blackened sheds at Bournemouth — past the Victorian houses of Beechey Road — a happy young man. In his pocket was his first wage packet of 30 shillings, double what he had been earning at the garage just the week before.

Dorset's first Christmas at war saw Doug Scott do his first firing turn — night shunting Bournemouth goods yard. In the early weeks of 1940, he notched up more firing turns, due to natural wastage and quicker promotion among Bournemouth men because of the war. 'As cleaners, if we had a firing turn we were paid nine shillings and sixpence a day on top of our normal pay. Each turn was recorded in a book at the shed and when you'd amassed 313 turns you got the fireman's rate of pay permanently.'

Doug first worked to Corfe Castle and Swanage after being transferred in June 1940 to Hamworthy Junction's shed which, like Swanage, was a sub-shed of Bournemouth. He moved to Hamworthy with fellow cleaner, Bernard Walton.

'Bernard would start his turn at 10pm and I'd go in at midnight. We'd keep the engines in steam and clean them for the crews to take over the next morning,' remembers Doug.

'There were five pairs of men at Hamworthy to crew the three locomotives based there, working from 5am through to 11pm. The crews would service Poole, Hamworthy Quay and Poole Quay as well as go down to Wareham, Corfe Castle and Swanage with the goods train and shunt the yards there.

'We used to have the "M7" Drummond 0-4-4T engines. After working down the branch, we'd change crews at Wareham and come back to Hamworthy light engine. There used to be a United Dairies depot at Corfe Castle then, just behind the 'down' platform. We used to load up the milk. Everyone used to help out with the work then — it was a great life. Very enjoyable. After being a cleaner at Bournemouth, doing firing turns down to Corfe Castle and Swanage was a real difference — a very pleasant trip.'

But, as Doug explains, his trips to Swanage were not always so good: 'On a dull and rainy winter's day the run into Swanage was very depressing. I can clearly recall passing the stone cottages and houses at Herston. It all looked so dismal and depressing. I used to get sick of the sight of it and yearned for the spring to come. But, on a sunny summer's day the trip down the branch was wonderful and thoroughly enjoyable.'

Above:
Held in the air like a toy, 62-ton Victorian 'M7' 0-4-4T No 30053 is carefully craned on to a low-loader at Felixstowe Docks on Wednesday 8 April 1987, prior to a two-day road journey home to Swanage. The 'M7' had completed a two-week voyage across the Atlantic after being purchased from the Steamtown Museum at Scranton, Pennsylvania, by the Drummond Locomotive Society. Following full restoration, she was due to steam out of Swanage during 1992. *Andrew P. M. Wright*

Monday 28 August 1939; just days before the outbreak of World War 2. 'Being a driver in those days was an elite job which people respected and looked up to. It was a job for life, if you wanted it — every young man's ambition, I suppose,' says Doug.

While waiting to be called by the Southern Railway, Doug worked at two Bournemouth garages. After finally being called by the Southern Railway Company, 17-year-old Doug Scott saw Mr Collins, the respected Bournemouth shedmaster and went to Southampton for his medical, before starting work as a cleaner at Bournemouth locomotive shed. Forty-eight years later, Stan Symes would retire from British Rail after a career that saw him travel one-and-a-half million

Left:
On a warm day in 1963, Swanage driver Jack Spicer enjoys the view as his 'M7' 0-4-4T No 30108 *Rosie* clatters over bridge No 21 and round the curve at Woodyhyde Farm — between Harman's Cross and Corfe Castle — with a two-coach mid-day train for Corfe Castle and Wareham. Built in 1904 at Nine Elms in London, *Rosie* was withdrawn in May 1964, and cut up for scrap in South Wales in October of that year. *Mike Esau*

Centre left:
Twenty-three years later, the same spot by Woodyhyde Farm had changed radically. Where *Rosie* once wheezed and clattered with her 'push-pull' trains has become a silent, weed-choked trackbed. Some 14 years after the tracks were lifted, this view looking towards Harman's Cross and Swanage was taken on the hazy summer morning of Friday 23 May 1986. In the foreground are the rotting remains of one of the many sleeper-built permanent way huts located along the line for the use of the track gangs. *Andrew P. M. Wright*

Bottom left:
Thanks to the grinding determination of Swanage Railway volunteers, by 1991 it was as though the Swanage branch had never been obliterated. Although *Rosie* has become so many razor blades, the sight and sound of a Victorian steam locomotive ambling through the Dorset countryside can still be enjoyed. Here, on Friday 10 May 1991, 1899-vintage LSWR 'T9' class 4-4-0 No 120 trundles over bridge 21 and round the curve past Woodyhyde Farm with an engineering train for Corfe Castle. *Andrew P. M. Wright*

47

Above:
Double-heading was a means of returning a locomotive back to its depot without creating a separate 'path' in the timetable and delaying other trains. Here, frequent branch visitor Drummond '700' class 0-6-0 No 30695 of Bournemouth MPD and 'M7' 0-4-4T No 30108 *Rosie*, haul a morning train past the pine trees of the Motala Kennels, Norden, with a Corfe Castle to Wareham train on Saturday 23 August 1958. This was where the scrap merchants lifting the branch track for British Rail stopped work and set up a stopblock in August 1972. *Sid C. Nash*

Right:
The same spot by the Motala Kennels on the sizzingly hot summer afternoon of Saturday 6 July 1990. With birch trees and choking undergrowth almost completely smothering what is left of the line, this is the furthest that BR now penetrates the Isle of Purbeck. The half-mile spur from Furzebrook is now used to store spare BP 100-tonne oil tankers for the huge Wytch Farm oil field north of Corfe Castle. *Andrew P. M. Wright*

Doug still remembers one of the regular drivers he worked with at Hamworthy Junction with affection. 'His name was Jesse Sherred — a real countryman rogue but a very likeable one. He used to live in Columbia Road, Bournemouth, and come to work with ferrets in his pockets. We were working a goods train down the branch one day and as we ran between Corfe Castle and Swanage — somewhere near Harman's Cross, I think — Jesse said that he was "dropping off". I didn't realise then what he meant.

'As the train slowed down to tackle the bank at Harman's Cross cutting — before going down to Swanage — he jumped off the footplate, clambered up the embankment, over the fence and into the trees. I couldn't believe it — I was left on the footplate alone. Since the train was going round the bend, the guard couldn't see the locomotive and Jesse leaping off.

'I took the train on down to Swanage to do the shunting. About an hour later he appeared walking down the track into the station with two rabbits over his arm. Jesse was a great rogue — but a genuine character, who really looked after me.

'He was a crack shot with a catapult too. He regularly used to go up to Haysom's stone yard at Swanage — just opposite the engine shed. There was always a pigeon pie at the end of it. He never seemed to miss.'

When Jesse went back to Bournemouth, Doug was joined at Hamworthy Junction by driver Wilf Selby, whose brother also worked on the railway. 'He was always as black as the ace of spades but a very nice chap. The job of a driver or fireman was never clean but poor old Wilf was the filthiest. I can remember him sitting on the footplate eating his doorstep sandwiches with hands absolutely black.

'I owe a lot to Wilf — he taught me a lot and drove the engine carefully, so there wasn't too much hard work for the fireman. That was different from some of the main line men.'

As a fireman based at Bournemouth, one of Doug's regular drivers was Fred Tollerfield, who lived in Boscombe. Together on the 'tank gang' or the 'lug-and-shove' as it was known, they used to take an 'M7' and two LSWR push-pull carriages down to Corfe Castle and Swanage.

'Fred was a short and tubby fellow with rose-bud cheeks and a round face. He always used to come to work with immaculate, freshly washed overalls and highly polished boots. Because he was rather tubby he couldn't get between the frames of the "M7" tanks to oil the motion, so I used to do it for him. I always used to start my turn a few minutes early and prepare the locomotive slowly. I found if preparation got behind schedule then the engine would steam badly all day.

'We were meant to use the compressed air system on the "M7s" when they were pushing the carriage set along the branch. The driver would be in the vestibule at the far end of the train, leaving the fireman alone on the footplate. The theory was the driver would control the locomotive regulator via compressed air. However, in practice it didn't work too well. Often the regulator would be either tight shut or wide open — there didn't seem to be any in-between.

'Because of this, most drivers pulled the pin out of the Westinghouse compressed air system. The driver still had control of the brake but he communicated with the fireman on the "M7" with bell codes. Most firemen working the branch knew the line so well that they didn't need bell codes anyway.

'From my point of view this was marvellous because it meant I was on the footplate alone and — for all intents and purposes — in charge of the locomotive. The fastest stretches on the branch were running towards Wareham from Furzebrook to Worgret Junction under Holme Lane and down the 1 in 78 and 1 in 76 gradients from Harman's Cross to Swanage.

'One problem we had in the early 1940s was coal. Because of the war, we didn't have the best steam coal, so had to make do with Kent coal. I'll always remember the smell of it — very recognisable. It was awful — really dusty. If you found a lump in the bunker that really was something.

'And then, of course, there was the blackout sheeting on the locomotives. No light was allowed to show from a steam locomotive in case it was spotted by enemy aircraft overhead and, therefore, become a potential target. There were covers over the lamps, windows and the cab sides. Working on the footplate at night was terribly hot and these covers made life very difficult for the crews. But they did stop you from being bombed or shot at, I suppose.'

After two full years' firing, Doug Scott was earning ten shillings and sixpence a day — an amount he considered to be good in the early 1940s, and certainly during wartime. While working at Bournemouth, he fired both in the two goods gangs as well as the push-and-pull gang — also known as the 'brush up and take water'.

'We used to work the now closed "Old Road" to Brockenhurst, via Wimborne and Ringwood — a run of over 30 miles or so — as well as doing odd turns down the Lymington

Right:
With just a brake van in tow, 'M7' 0-4-4 No 30112 runs light engine between New Barn and the A351 Nursery bridge on Saturday 8 August 1953. Built in 1900, the non 'push-pull' fitted 'M7' is bound for Corfe Castle and Wareham after working a goods train down to Swanage earlier in the day. For many years there was a daily goods train to Swanage but by 1963 it only ran on Tuesdays and Thursdays and on Monday 4 October 1965, the service was abandoned completely.
R. R. Bowler/
courtesy of Mike Smith collection

Below:
Where's the railway gone? Unbelievably, it's still there — just. The same position as 'M7' No 30112 in the previous picture and looking towards Swanage but 30 years later in July 1982 — just 10 years after the BR track was lifted. This is what the Swanage Railway volunteers had to contend with when they cleared the two-mile section of disused trackbed between Herston and Harman's Cross in 1985.
Andrew P. M. Wright

and Swanage branches. There were 12 pairs of men at Bournemouth to cover the roster — six for the early shifts, with a start time that could be anywhere between 2am and 11am, and six for the late turn. We worked two trains to Swanage then — one from Bournemouth Central and one from Bournemouth West.

'The Swanage and Bournemouth "push-pull" crews got on very well. We both had a job to do and they had their world — like a separate little community and we had ours. Push-and-pull work down to Swanage wasn't everybody's cup of tea but I quite liked it.'

Doug will always remember one spring day in 1944 when he and his driver came face to face with one of the brains behind the largest maritime invasion — and probably the biggest military gamble — the world has ever known on Swanage seafront of all places.

'Wilf Selby and I had worked a goods down from Bournemouth to Swanage from Corfe Castle and Wareham. We'd been told that several special trains were due in Swanage but weren't given any more information. When we reached Swanage about 10am, we shunted the yard and made sure that everything was out of the way. We were light engine in the station loop when a special train arrived in the bay. Then another came in and ran into the neighbouring goods shed siding.'

On board were D-Day Allied Commanders Arthur Tedder and Bertram Ramsay as well as General Bernard Montgomery — the victor of El Alamein. They were in Swanage with General Eisenhower, Prime Minister Winston Churchill and King George VI to watch rehearsals at Studland for the D-Day Allied landings in Normandy.

'There was a lot of top brass on the station that morning. We saw Montgomery and Eisenhower and knew something was on but had no idea of the impending invasion of France.

'After we'd finished our shunting — and while waiting for a path back up to Wareham — my driver and I had the choice of either going to the Railway Hotel opposite the stop-blocks for our usual pint or a walk down the town and along the seafront to stretch our legs and get some air.

'Since it was a fine day we thought we'd walk along the front. There were concrete anti-tank traps along the sea wall and a line of rusting scaffolding in the water. We were walking along when we were amazed to see Montgomery walking on his own towards us. He was calming throwing his maroon beret in the air and catching it. Wilf and I just couldn't believe it.'

The residents of Swanage had been told by the authorities to open their windows that day and keep them open until asked to close them.

'Later, over lunchtime we realised why. We were steaming back from Swanage to Bournemouth with a rake of box vans and open five-plank wagons, when we heard something unusual between Harman's Cross and Corfe Castle. It was the muffled sound of bombing on the other side of the Purbeck Hills at Studland. Apparently, American B24 Liberators and B17 Flying Fortresses as well as British planes were practising saturation bombing on the heaths in preparation for D-Day.'

The irregular working hours that Doug hated so much — and which were and are part and parcel of railway life — were to prove the end of his railway career. After complaining of severe indigestion and lack of energy, the railway doctor diagnosed the young fireman as having acute dispepsia, brought on by his shift work. In late 1945, Doug Scott was released from the Southern Railway and went on to farm work and then a career in aircraft engineering.

'I was sad to leave. I didn't want to but I was ill and just wasn't getting better. I enjoyed my time on the Southern Railway because of the people I was working with. There was a great team spirit even though the job was physically tough and exhausting.'

Below:
Miracles do happen — and here's living proof. On the warm summer afternoon of Sunday 7 July 1991, Midland Railway '1F' 0-6-0T No 41708 of 1880 tackles the 1 in 76 gradient up to Harman's Cross and is about to pass under the A351 Nursery road bridge with a four-coach 15.40 train from Swanage.
Andrew P. M. Wright

The Fireman's Tale

5

'On the last train of the day from Wareham to Swanage, we managed to complete the ten-mile trip in 17 minutes, instead of the usual 22 — reaching the station in time to nip across into the nearby Conservative Club for a quick pint.'

Stan Brown

Below:
Ex-Swanage branch fireman from 1944-1947, Stan Brown is reunited with LSWR 'T9' class 4-4-0 No 120 for the first time since 1950. Built in 1899, the 'T9' was a regular performer at Swanage from World War 1 up until 1960. Stan saw No 30120 become a victim of the Luftwaffe when it was viciously straffed by two Me109s at Wool station on Saturday 28 November 1942. No 120 is on a 10-year loan to the Swanage Railway from the National Railway Museum at York. *Andrew P. M. Wright*

In the dying days of the Southern Railway, a young fireman restlessly sits on the footplate of his grimy 'M7' tank locomotive at Bournemouth shed as his driver laboriously recites yet another passage from the Bible to him.

It is the autumn of 1947 and 23-year old Stan Brown has just left the cosy familiarity of the Swanage branch line for the main line world of Bournemouth. He takes a deep and resigned sigh and looks out of the cab as his driver continues to drone on — and the Bournemouth Belle sweeps past into the station from London. As Ted 'Holy Joe' Purchase studiously and piously recites even more New Testament verse, poor old Stan closes his ears. How he wishes he was back on Swanage's familiar 'push-and-pull' trains with his regular driver Bob Mitchell.

Six years before in 1941, Stan must have felt Adolf Hitler had something against him personally because the Dorset teenager was bombed out of his Bristol aircraft factory by the Luftwaffe on no less than two occasions. 'I thought the railways would be a safer place to work,' grins Stan looking back. His wartime years spent working the main line from

Dorchester and then the Swanage branch were not uneventful — and sometimes anything but safe. He was firing a heavy ammunition train at Southampton when he was caught in the tunnel by the Central Station during an air raid. Although Stan and his driver did not know it at the time, a German bomb had blocked the tunnel entrance behind them.

Stan Brown has been on petrol trains when their axleboxes caught fire — and he was very nearly the target of a vicious Luftwaffe attack on LSWR 'T9' 4-4-0 No 120 at Wool station.

Nearly 50 years after that eventful day in November 1942, Stan was able to come face to face with the same veteran Victorian locomotive at Swanage, thanks to a 10-year loan to the Swanage Railway's Purbeck Line from the National Railway Museum at York.

The Southern Railway's 'T9' No 120, as she was then, was stationary and blowing off by the 'down' starter signal at Wool station — waiting for the 'right away' to Moreton. The locomotive was hauling the regular Brockenhurst to Dorchester freight working, when the Luftwaffe launched their attack at lunchtime on Saturday 28 November 1942.

Young Dorchester cleaner Stan Brown was just a few hundred yards away from the 'T9' that day and saw the sudden attack happen in front of his eyes. 'I was firing a "down" freight from Wareham with Harry Davis, when we came running into the station around 12.45pm. A few hundred yards ahead was the "T9" at a stand by the Ship Inn as she waited for the line to Moreton to be cleared.'

Wool's station was packed with hundreds of servicemen from Bovington Camp waiting to catch the Saturday lunchtime servicemen's train from Wool to Poole and Bournemouth West. 'Suddenly, I heard the growl of aircraft and looking up into the bright sky I saw two German Messerschmitt Me109s flying in low over the station from the north. It was a beautifully sunny Saturday and they'd obviously seen the "T9" blowing off by the station's

Above:
Stan Brown's regular goods engine — Drummond '700' class 0-6-0 No 30695 — shunts a rake of empty clay wagons out of the loop at Corfe Castle station and into the East Hill cutting one afternoon in March 1956. She then ran back up to Eldon's Siding at Norden and then Furzebrook sidings. A familiar sight on the branch for many years, No 30695 was often the station pilot at Swanage on summer Saturdays. Designed by Dugald Drummond in 1897, she was withdrawn by BR in December 1962, stored at Eastleigh locomotive works and cut up there in May 1963. *Dr Gerald Siviour*

Left:
The undergrowth-choked cutting through the Purbeck Hills at Corfe Castle on Saturday 4 July 1987, looking towards the station. The tall 'down' home signal post can just be discerned amongst the trees to the right. It's hard to believe that 120-ton 'West Country' and 'Battle of Britain' class Bulleid Pacific express steam locomotives ran through here. Until Dorset County Council chose an outer eastern route for the much-needed and long-awaited Corfe Castle by-pass, railway opponents wanted to take the road over the trackbed. *Andrew P. M. Wright*

53

starter signal as she waited for the "right-away" from the signalman.'

One of the German cannon shells exploded on the footplate. Dorchester driver, Harry 'Nobby' Clark, sustained cannon shell shrapnel wounds to the back of his head, whilst fireman, Doug Keegan, had shrapnel wounds in his buttocks. The injured crew — writhing in pain — were quickly despatched to the nearby military hospital at Bovington Camp.

'The locomotive had been riddled with bullets and cannon shells from end to end. She was losing water like a sieve and making a lot of noise because her hydrostatic lubricator steam pipe had been severed in the attack. Water was pouring through a bullet hole that had punctured the firebox. She had sustained numerous other hits to her smokebox and boiler cladding, as well as to her cab and tender.'

Stan Brown was born in Wool. His father worked on the Swanage branch line from the 1930s — a track ganger responsible for the five-mile stretch between Corfe Castle and Worgret Junction, working with the likes of Alfie Allingham and Fred King. After twice being bombed out of his Bristol aircraft factory, where he was a fitter, 17-year-old Stan returned to Dorset and took the advice of his father — 'get a job on the railway'.

Stan's first pay packet as a cleaner at Dorchester locomotive shed was just £1/11/6.

Facing page, top:
On the hot afternoon of Saturday 11 June 1966, grimy BR Standard Class 4 2-6-4T No 80138 accelerates up the 1 in 78 gradient between Herston and New Barn with its two-coach train from Swanage to Corfe Castle and Wareham. During the final months of branch steam traction in 1966, trains were frequently composed of a late 1940s Southern Railway Bulleid coach in green with a mid-1950s BR Mk 1 coach, often in maroon livery.
Tim Stephens

Facing page, bottom:
On a muggy July morning, ex-Midland Railway '1F' 0-6-0T No 41708 of 1880 tackles the same gradient between Herston Halt and New Barn as No 80138 did a quarter of a century ago, with the four-coach 11.00 Swanage to Harman's Cross train on Sunday 21 July 1991.
Andrew P. M. Wright

Centre left:
Rarely photographed, veteran driver Jack Spicer allowed Swanage photographer Chris Phillips to take this picture of him leaning from the cab of an ex-LMS Ivatt tank while waiting between branch trains at Wareham in the summer of 1966. Jack was only weeks from retirement after a railway career that stretched back to the 1920s. *Chris Phillips*

Left:
The face of a Swanage driver in 1990. Clive Groome leans from the cab of 1924-built Great Eastern Railway-designed 'N7' class 0-6-2T No 69621 at Swanage station between departures for Herston halt and Harman's Cross. An ex-BR driver from the 1960s, Clive now runs footplate classes on the Swanage Railway as well as other preserved railways.
Andrew P. M. Wright

If he had a firing turn then he was paid one shilling a day extra on top of that. He was to stay based at Dorchester until promotion as a fireman took him to Swanage in September 1944 — when the Allies were staging their Arnhem 'Bridge too far' landings in Holland.

Stan still remembers the remarkable sight of the vast armada of planes that flew over Dorset the night before the historic but costly Allied D-Day landings in Normandy on 6 June 1944. 'I was firing the midnight goods working from Eastleigh to Dorchester. Passing through Wareham around 12.45am, I looked out from the blackout sheets covering the footplate and couldn't believe what I saw. It was a beautiful moonlit night and the sky was filled with thousands of planes towing gliders over to France. It was a fantastic sight.'

The large goods yard at Wareham used to act as an overspill area for the storage of tanks, ammunition and coal from Wool yard — serving the Bovington Ministry of Defence Camp — as well as the sidings at Holton Heath. They served the huge Royal Navy Cordite Factory that supplied hundreds of thousands of shells to the Royal Navy during the war.

While a cleaner at Dorchester, Stan used to fire permanent way ash trains that visited Corfe Castle and Swanage on Saturday nights to build up areas of slippage or subsidence along the trackside — as well as maintain the ash cess.

'The New Barn embankment was a favourite location because of its unstable bank, which had a 10mph speed limit imposed on all trains. We'd normally use a Drummond "700" locomotive and our regular engine was No 700 — later numbered 30700 after nationalisation into British Railways.

'As the driver and fireman, we had the easy job because we'd sit on the footplate drinking tea and watching them hard at work — just moving the train forward when asked. We'd run down from Wareham after the last train on the Saturday evening and be working on the line throughout the night before the first "up" train from Swanage on the Sunday morning.'

Stan still remembers a special wartime train carrying tanks from Hamworthy to Wool that not only caused concern at Wareham station — but to the guard, as well.

'We had a double load of 12 tanks on and had a job to get the "L10" locomotive moving at Hamworthy Junction. Once we got the train underway, we daren't slow down in case we came to a halt and couldn't get going again.

'The platforms at Wareham were cleared of people because the width of tanks breached the usual clearances. We rattled through at quite a speed to gain momentum up the bank. I remember we took a chance and ran under the three-arched road bridge by Worgret Junction at 40mph instead of the 10mph we should have done. The guard was frightened we'd take the bridge — and his brake van — with us as we ran through, but we didn't.

'We ran the whole way tender first to Wool and were relieved that we managed to get there in one piece — or at all. I didn't put my shovel down during the whole trip and had lost half a box of fire by the time we reached our destination.'

As a Lance Corporal in the Home Guard at Wool, Stan was charged with looking after the unit's 2lb anti-tank gun. In July 1944, he spent a week down at Swanage station during its fund-raising 'Salute the Soldier' week. Moving to Swanage as a fireman on the branch's push-and-pull service in September 1944, Stan's pay was increased to five pounds and thirteen shillings a week.

'I lodged with one of the branch drivers, Sam Boyland, and his wife at his house in Hillsea Road at Swanage. Sam's regular fireman used to be Stan "Enoch" Hawkes, who moved to Swanage from Cornwall, married a WAAF and later left Swanage when I did, moving out of the area. I replaced Bill King, who went to Bournemouth, and worked with Bob Mitchell. Fireman Jack Stockley was paired with Jack Spicer. Jack Stockley's father, Bill, worked as a track ganger at Corfe Castle.

'There were three turns at Swanage then — the early (4am to 12 noon), the middle (10am to 6pm) and late (3pm to 11pm). I liked branch line work. Driver Bob Mitchell was a smashing man to work with. Occasionally, I'd do a turn with Jack Spicer who could be rather awkward at times. He always used to bring three packets of 20 Players cigarettes to work every day and he was always to be seen with a cigarette in his mouth and clutching an oil can in one hand and a rag in the other.

'While Jack was rather old-fashioned and a worrier, Bob Mitchell was always calm and collected. He was very laid back, had a sense of humour and, I think, had been at Swanage since the 1930s. Bob knew his job and was certainly more confident than most — he didn't used to worry — but he could speak his mind if he wanted to.

'The generation gap between young firemen and drivers, perhaps in their 50s or 60s, was always a problem on the railway. But, you could always speak to Bob and he'd always help you. Jack wouldn't. He could be impatient — helpful one day and then not very co-operative the next. Bob was patient and taught me a lot about the job. I owe him a great deal.

Facing page, top:

On a fine summer's evening in 1963 — and just months from withdrawal — elderly Victorian 'M7' 0-4-4T No 30129 clanks her way round the curve between the A351 Catseye Bridge and the Motala Kennels at Norden with a two-coach Maunsell 'push-pull' train from Swanage and Corfe Castle to Wareham. Built in 1911, 'M7' No 30129 was fitted for push-pull working in 1925 and spent many years based at Yeovil. Moving to Bournemouth in April 1963, No 30129 was withdrawn that November and cut up a month later at Eastleigh. *Mike Esau*

Facing page, bottom:

With the wheezing 'M7' locomotives chugging their way through the Isle of Purbeck just a memory, the trackbed between the Catseye Bridge and the Motala Kennels at Norden lies silent and overgrown on the humid afternoon of Saturday 6 July 1991. Two short sidings for anti-aircraft rail-mounted guns veered off the north side of the branch by the Motala Kennels during World War 2. Laid in 1940 and 1941, they were taken up in 1946. *Andrew P. M. Wright*

'Sam Boyland was a real character and used to love a drink. I was his fireman on the last train of the day from Wareham to Swanage one evening, when we managed to do the 10-mile trip in 17 minutes instead of the usual 22 minutes. That included the one-minute stop to exchange the single-line tablets at Corfe Castle. We got to Swanage in time to nip into the nearby Railway Hotel or the Conservative Club by the station for a quick pint of beer before it closed.

'Bournemouth-passed firemen Sid Gittings and Jock Hapgood used to bring trains down the branch regularly during the war. Hamworthy Junction worked down to Corfe Castle and Swanage, too, although most of their work was on the clay and freight trains down the branch.

'We used to change locomotives with a Bournemouth crew every day at Wareham — a definite disadvantage, because we could never keep our engine clean. The "M7s" at Bournemouth were always rather mucky, so it was great when we were later given a regular engine which we kept polished. Mine used to be good old 107 (later given the number 30107 after nationalisation). We also had 052, and 111 — known as "Lord Nelson" to the crews — amongst others.

'The "M7s" never gave us any trouble, so long as they were maintained regularly and had their tubes cleaned. Firing them wasn't hard work, so long as you kept a foot and a half of fire in the box and kept it light and bright coming up the hill from Swanage. I used to put the injectors on after we passed the gas works sidings at Victoria Avenue.

'Bob Mitchell was an excellent driver, because he didn't drive the locomotive so you'd use a lot of coal. Sam Boyland would burn more because he used to like turning on the speed, unlike Bob. Jack Spicer could be very heavy-handed at times.

'I'd say Bob and I wouldn't use more than four and a half hundredweight of coal between Swanage and Wareham with a push-pull set in tow. Once you reached Harman's Cross, went over the napp and on to the "plain", as we called it, you'd coast all the way to Afflington and then down into Corfe Castle to build up the fire and water.

'The same would be true running out of Corfe, past Eldon's Sidings at Norden and on up to Furzebrook. After shutting off on the summit by the clay sidings, you'd run the three miles down to Worgret Junction.'

Stan does however remember one eventful trip on the branch with his trusty 'M7' and a two-coach LSWR push-pull carriage set on a train near Herston. 'Bob was able to drag her up as far as New Barn but there we had to come to a halt because, with only one cylinder working, she was running like a kangaroo. That was a very rough ride. I had to run back to Swanage with the single-line tablet and get the Hamworthy goods engine — shunting the goods at the station — to rescue poor old 107 and push her up to Corfe Castle.

'The Hamworthy men did the majority of goods turns down the branch during the war — including the clay train to Furzebrook and Norden, which they'd run round via the loop at Corfe Castle.

'The Bournemouth push-and-pull men also took trains down to Swanage. They'd come down with an early morning working and then haul the 7.15am workers' train up to Corfe, Wareham and back to Bournemouth. We'd work the 5.15am from Swanage to Hamworthy, which also called at Holton Heath. There was also a Swanage branch train that ended up at Bournemouth West station.

'In the evenings during the war we'd work the 5.15pm Swanage to Wareham train which met the 5.15pm Bournemouth Central to Swanage train. We'd then go on to Wool.'

After three years and three months at Swanage, further promotion took Stan Brown to Bournemouth shed and a job with the shed's push-and-pull gang in late 1947. 'I was sad to leave Swanage and the people I knew and had worked with because it had a real family atmosphere. They were a friendly little crowd.'

As his time at Bournemouth went on, the commuting from his home at Wool across to the conurbation every day and night began to take its toll and Stan left British Railways in 1951.

'I'm not sure what the old drivers I worked with at Swanage during the war would think of the Swanage Railway now, though. I think Bob Mitchell would like it. He'd have been sad to see the branch killed off in the way it was. He was that kind of man.

'Jack Spicer would too, although he probably wouldn't admit it. As for Sam Boyland, I think he'd like it — but only if there was a pint in it!' grins Stan.

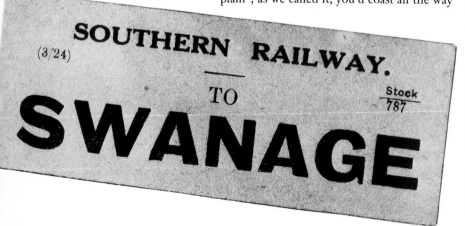

The Branch Driver's Tale

6

'I opened the regulator wide open and we ploughed through it. The snow was the height of the chimney and I just hoped we wouldn't come off the rails. It was freezing — snow flying everywhere.'

Fred Norman

It is mid-February 1944, and 18-year-old Fred Norman walks slowly along a quiet residential road in Swanage, furtively looking down at the Pullman train standing in the station platform, before being hastily shooed off by a nervous Grenadier Guard on sentry duty.

Little did Fred know that 33 years later he would drive one of the last diesel trains out of that station platform on the afternoon of Saturday 1 January 1972; witness the starvation and destruction of the branch line he would spend so much of his life working on, before seeing it slowly rebuilt in front of his eyes.

Forty-six years after starting as a cleaner with the Southern Railway at Bournemouth, Fred ended his career in late 1991 racing up and down the London to Weymouth main line at the controls of the hi-tech Class 442 Wessex Electrics — and having the unexpected honour of driving the first passenger-carrying InterCity 125 train down to Poole in the summer of 1991.

'The closure was a disaster. Politics closed the Swanage line and it has been politics that tried to stop the railway coming back,' muses Fred wryly from his house which is just a few yards from the rebuilt Purbeck Line on the outskirts of Swanage.

Fred has seen Swanage's railway come full circle over the past 50 years — and all from his railway allotment that he has known since a child. From that patch of turnips, rhubarb, cabbages and onions up by the distant signal on the outskirts of the Dorset seaside town, he has seen the branch railway line thrive in the 1940s, decline in the 1950s, wither and die in the 1960s, be closed and torn up in the 1970s — and relaid in the 1980s; all in front of his vegetable patch.

Fred was born in Croydon in 1927 but did not return to the 'ancestral seat' in the Purbecks, as he calls it, until 1938. Leaving school two years later at the age of 14, Fred started working as a paper boy for the station bookstall at Swanage — H. G. Cook & Son.

However, Fred's duties also took him and his trusty bicycle further afield — on the push-pull train to Wareham before the five-mile ride to Wool, where he would deliver more papers. 'Having a bicycle during the war was a great advantage — but it also meant that you were in great demand and I was soon roped into being a messenger-boy for the Home Guard in Swanage.'

Working from the town's station as he did, Fred witnessed at first hand some of the antics of the branch line's Home Guard as well.

'Cecil Collins — a porter, porter/guard and then finally a guard at Swanage — frequently used to saunter off home for his tea after his turn came to an end, take his time, and then turn up late at the station for the Home Guard parade. He used to be told off for that, as well as coming to the Home Guard nights with a mixture of his railway and Home Guard uniform on.

'The hit BBC Television comedy *Dad's Army* really is a pale shadow of what went on in the railway Home Guard at Swanage during the war. As well as Mr Nobbs — a real Captain Mainwaring type — being the captain of the outfit, driver Sam Boyland was a sergeant.

Below:
Driver Fred Norman (left) meets ex-Swanage branch fireman Stan Brown (right) for the first time since 1950 — in May 1991. The pair last saw each other at Bournemouth Depot in 1950, just before Stan left BR. Joining the Southern Railway in 1945 as a cleaner at Bournemouth, Fred Norman fired and drove trains down to Corfe Castle and Swanage from the late 1940s. He had the distinction of driving the last timetabled train out of Swanage on the last day of operation — New Year's Day 1972.
Andrew P. M. Wright

Right:
Trains pass at Corfe Castle station on Saturday 8 August 1953. 'M7' 0-4-4T No 30106 simmers at the 'down' platform with its LSWR 'push-pull' set, waiting to leave for Swanage. In the 'up' platform, unrebuilt 'Battle of Britain' Bulleid Pacific No 34109 *Sir Trafford Leigh Mallory* waits to leave with a train for London Waterloo. This rare view was taken from the old signalbox on the 'down' platform. Demolished in 1956 and moved to the 'up' platform, the new box was built as an extension to the porter's lobby. *R. R. Bowler/ courtesy of the Mike Smith collection*

Below:
Corfe Castle station lies silent and awaiting the Swanage Railway's track-relaying train on the afternoon of Tuesday 6 April 1989. Volunteers have cleared the 14 years of undergrowth and weeds from the trackbed and the platforms. Anti-railway protestors lobbying an inner-eastern route for the much-needed and long-awaited Corfe by-pass wanted the new road to demolish the Victorian station and use the trackbed. However, Dorset County Council has voted to support an outer-eastern route.
Andrew P. M. Wright

'Sam had seen service in Mesopotamia during World War 1. Fellow driver, Bob Mitchell, was a corporal. Driver Jack Spicer had recently moved down to the branch from Dover in Kent and never used to wear his regulation Army boots, because he said he had bad feet.

'Another member of Swanage station's Home Guard, and a real character, was George Howe, who worked in the goods shed. He always used to turn up for Home Guard duty late and with his little white dog.

That was despite being told repeatedly not to. It was the spitting image of the symbol on the His Master's Voice records of the time — that's why I still remember it.'

The finest hour of the railway Home Guard at Swanage was in February 1944. They were called in to help with security when King George, Generals Eisenhower and Montgomery as well as Winston Churchill and other 'top brass' travelled to Swanage to watch vital rehearsals for the D-Day landings.

'I can remember slowly walking along Gilbert Road overlooking the main station and platform and trying to get a glimpse of the special trains and what was going on. But, the sentries wouldn't even allow me to walk on the station side of the road, they were that touchy.'

However, as well as helping with security, Swanage station's Home Guard was charged with emptying the latrines on board the special trains. Sergeant Sam Boyland, being a senior member, had the 'honour' of emptying the King's commode — and was not allowed to forget it for years afterwards.

Above:
A rare view of the Southern Railway's Home Guard at Swanage early in World War 2. All signs naming the station have been taken down in the event of the expected German invasion. To the far right is Swanage's stationmaster, Mr Nobbs. Sitting on the Bren gun carrier to the far left is parcels clerk Charlie Callen with chief booking clerk Dicky Dawe in the front driving seat — above the 55. *Courtesy of Les Hayward*

Centre left:
'M7' 0-4-4T No 30107 drifts into Corfe Castle station loop with a late afternoon train from Swanage during the summer of 1963. Built in 1905, No 30107 was the very last 'M7' to work the Swanage branch on Saturday 9 May 1964. Taken from the station's end-loading dock, this view shows the layout of the compact but well-designed goods yard. Moving right, off the headshunt lead sidings to the end-loading dock, the goods shed and Pullman camping coaches and finally the coal siding. *Mike Esau*

Bottom left:
A tangled mess of wild trees and undergrowth once blocked this view. With the 'down' track only just relaid into Corfe station, LSWR Drummond 'T9' 4-4-0 No 120 of 1899 gingerly runs into Corfe Castle station on the afternoon of Friday 10 May 1991, to collect an engineering train and return it to Swanage. With the goods shed line laid to the right, the volunteers still have to lay the 'up' loop line into the station, as well as the sidings to the end-loading dock and the coal siding. *Andrew P. M. Wright*

Top:
Special enthusiasts' trains from London were frequent visitors to the Swanage branch before the end of all BR Southern Region steam in 1967. With passengers excitedly leaning out of every available window, the LCGB's nine-coach 'Dorset Belle' railtour winds its way past what is now Pondarosa Farm at Harman's Cross just after midday, en route from Corfe Castle to Swanage on a chilly Sunday 27 February 1966.
Tim Stephens

Above:
Taken from the same spot as the previous picture, the scene has changed dramatically with the sprouting of Pondarosa Farm. On a gloriously warm and sunny day in July 1991, ex-Midland Railway '1F' 0-6-0T No 41708 of 1880 clatters down the 1 in 76 gradient with the 15.00 Harman's Cross to Swanage train on Sunday 21 July 1991.
Andrew P. M. Wright

At the end of four years working at Swanage station, getting to know the staff and riding the push-and-pull trains to Wareham when on the Wool newspaper round, Fred decided to join the Southern Railway with the coming of peace in June 1945.

After a year as a young cleaner undergoing the rigours of the hierarchy at Bournemouth shed, he was transferred to Hamworthy Junction in 1946. He was to stay there for four years before making his first professional sorties down to Corfe Castle and Swanage. Returning to Bournemouth in 1950, Fred started work on the push-and-pull gang which ran the passenger service on the 'Old Road' to Ringwood and Brockenhurst, as well as doing odd trips down the Lymington and Swanage branches.

In Coronation year, 1953, Fred started work at Swanage — a sub-shed of Bournemouth. His take-home pay was around £7 a week. He will always remember the subject of railway pay for footplate crews on the branch, because Swanage driver Sam Boyland had a rather unusual way of equating pay increases. 'One year we had a five and a half per cent increase in pay. I quickly worked out how much extra money we'd get by doing a sum with a piece of chalk on the side of the "M7's" bunker. I'd then tell Sam and he'd sit there for a minute, musing to himself, before

replying. Then, he'd say in a bright voice, "That's four and a half pints of beer". He equated everything into pints of beer!'

After doing 280 turns as a 'passed' fireman, Fred Norman went for examination as a driver at Bournemouth and passed. It was during the summer of 1963 that the first BR Standard Class 4 2-6-4T steam locomotives, designed in 1950, and the LMS Ivatt 2-6-2T, dating from 1946, started to appear on the branch after being ousted by electrification around London.

'We were glad to see the back of the old "M7s"', remembers Fred. 'They could be very light-footed in wet weather. I can remember as a fireman working an early morning Swanage to Corfe train and sliding to a halt up at New Barn. The sanding gear on the "M7s" never seemed to work, so if you did manage to coax it into working, it was a miracle. And then it would only work for half a mile or so before packing up just when you needed it.

'On this early morning train we just weren't getting any adhesion up the bank to Harman's Cross at all. So, I was forced to get out, put some sand from the boxes on a shovel and sprinkle it on the rails in front of the train as the locomotive slowly moved up behind me. Another trick was to use fine ballast.

'The "M7s" weren't in the same league as the Standard tanks. The BR Standards were built for speed and hauling long commuter trains off the Eastern Region into the London terminus stations but were wasteful of coal and water.

'When I actually got on a Standard Class 4 engine, I couldn't believe it — it was a completely different world to the one we'd known. The footplate was wide enough to play a game of football on and it had a speedometer, something we never had on the old "M7s."

'The speed and the acceleration of the electric-like Standards used to scare Jack Spicer. He was used to judging speed on the old "M7s" by the sound of the locomotive and the way it was moving. That just didn't work with the new locomotives.

'When on an "M7" you didn't only have to worry about keeping steam, controlling the regulator and the Westinghouse pump but also the danger of the reverser falling off. A grand time was had by all with all that lot happening,' recalls Fred with a wry smile.

'But, the "M7s" weren't too bad when you got the fire right. The only disadvantage was that crews had to clean the firebox of ash and clinker by shovelling it all out through the firehole door by hand at the end of a turn.

'That was a messy and tiring business, especially during the summer when it could take you up to half an hour to complete. The Standards and Ivatts had dropgrates, which made disposal duties an absolute joy in comparison.

'Swanage never had the best coal — it always went to the main line. Sometimes we had to work with Kent coal which was appalling because it was like fine gunpowder. It burnt like earth and felt like potting compost.'

One 'M7' — regular branch performer No 30107 and the last 'M7' to run into Swanage and Corfe Castle — proved her weight in gold during the big freeze of 1962/1963. It had snowed heavily on the evening of Saturday 29 December 1962, and by the following morning the branch was covered in snow, embankments indistinguishable from cuttings. 'Jimmy Hunt was on duty in Swanage signalbox that morning. He called me up to say the booked driver for the 10.15 from Swanage to Wareham, Jock Hapgood, hadn't been able to get to work from his home in Bournemouth. I agreed to come into work and do his turn for him.'

Not knowing if they would reach Corfe Castle let alone Wareham, Driver Fred Norman gingerly started out of Swanage at the controls of 'M7' No 30107 — expecting the worst.

'As we plodded up to New Barn and Harman's Cross, the snow got deeper and deeper and more compact. Steaming over the "summit" at Harman's Cross we continued across the "plain" to Afflington and Corfe Castle. Rounding the bend past Woodyhyde Farm at about 40 miles an hour, Afflington Bridge came into view and I saw the most amazing sight. The whole of the stone arch was filled with snow except for between 18in and 2ft at the crown of the arch.

'I just opened the regulator and we ploughed through it. The snow was the height of the chimney and I just hoped that we didn't come off the rails. Snow was flying everywhere and falling into the cab. The odd thing was that the sound of the locomotive motion and the beat of the exhaust was absorbed and muffled by the snow. There was none of the usual clanking sounds — we were almost silent apart from the sound of the snow hitting the train.'

Bob Inman, the signalman at Corfe Castle that day, could not believe his eyes as the train came down the gradient and into the loop. There was hardly any train noise at all, just a giant plume of white as the 'M7' determinedly ploughed its way through the snow.

Above:

Swanage beach was a favourite spot for locomotive crews resting between trains. Sticking out amongst hoards of 1960s sun worshippers and excited children with their buckets and spades, driver Jock Hapgood and fireman Ken Hordle take a break in the sun on the promenade. Ken's father, Sid, was a shunter and acting foreman at Wareham station for 45 years. Joining BR as a cleaner in 1953, Ken is now driving hi-tech 100mph Class 442 main line 'Wessex Electric' trains between London and Weymouth.
Courtesy of Ken Hordle

Left:

The driver and fireman of ex-LMS Ivatt 2-6-2T No 41238 water their locomotive at Swanage's coaling dock, before leaving with a train bound for Corfe Castle and Wareham on Thursday 11 June 1964. In the foreground is the 50ft turntable with beyond the Northbrook Road bridge, the air raid shelter, extensive goods yard and carriage sidings. *John Scrace*

Below left:

Against all the odds, and proving the sceptics wrong, the classic lines of an Ivatt steam locomotive could be once again admired at Swanage station's coaling dock in 1989. On loan from the Severn Valley Railway, Class 2 Ivatt 2-6-0 No 46443 takes a lunch break between hauling trains from Swanage to Harman's Cross on Friday 26 May 1989. Built at Crewe in 1950, No 46443 spent her career working in the Midlands and Lancashire before being withdrawn by BR in early 1967.
Andrew P. M. Wright

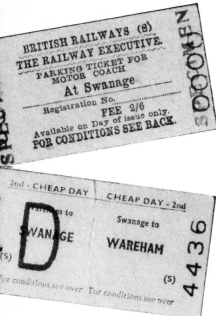

The year of President Kennedy's assassination — 1963 — was the last summer that branch trains were hauled by the old 'M7' tanks. As Fred Norman remembers, they were on their last legs. 'They never were well maintained, so by the early 1960s were at the end of their useful lives. Built at the turn of the century, they were due for replacement by the Southern Railway in the late 1930s but the outbreak of World War 2 put paid to that.'

By the beginning of May 1964, the last 'M7' had wheezed its way asthmatically down the branch before going on the scrap line at Eastleigh Works and then transferred to South Wales for scrapping in the dying weeks of 1964.

'We had heard rumours we were going to get the Standard "4" tanks and the Ivatts, but I never believed them until I actually saw one standing in front of me.

'The Standards really went like the wind once you opened the regulator and let them go up the bank to Harman's Cross. The "M7s" and Standard Class 4s were a complete world apart — like comparing a carthorse and a racehorse.'

Fred Norman still remembers when driver Jack Spicer and fireman Ken Hordle changed from an old 'M7' to a state-of-the-art Standard Class 4 engine at Swanage one evening.

'They got off the Drummond tank, walked across the platform to the bay where a Standard was waiting to work a train back to Wareham. It was a different world as they climbed into the spacious cab. The Standards had everything a crew could want — a steam brake, an accurate and dependable "bacon slicer" reverser, controls for the driver and fireman on separate sides, as well as a blower that worked properly, drop grates and speedometers.

'It was amazing — like getting on the London Underground and going to the moon. Off Victorian technology one minute and on to a modern steam locomotive that was designed to last into the 1980s. We'd never seen anything like it.'

But, it took the older drivers, like Jack Spicer and Jock Hapgood, quite a time to get used to the new technology after over 20 years with the old 'M7s'.

'Jack's style of working was very 1920s. He tended to worry a lot and would always be carrying his oilcan in one hand and a rag in the other. Over the years the attitudes of drivers to their firemen changed. I've always said that no matter how good the locomotive or driver, they are only as good as the fireman. Not having a good fireman is like not having petrol in your car.

'The best locomotive for the Swanage branch in my book was the LMS 2-6-2 Ivatt tank. They were marvellous engines to work with and ideal for branch line work, because they were light on their feet, responsive and economic. With their four-foot grates they could burn anything but were controllable. They were beautiful machines and had a sunshine roof, sliding windows, injector controls on one side of the cab for the fireman.

'With an Ivatt, you could run from Swanage to Wareham and back on one tank of water and have plenty left over. The Standard Class 4s were much more wasteful on water with their larger water tanks, coal bunker and firebox area.

'I used to play cricket with Driver Jock Hapgood in Corfe yard between trains. It would be the locomotive crew versus the rest of the staff. At Swanage, we'd spend two weeks on the push-and-pull service and the third on goods work up and down the branch.'

Fred still remembers with amusement an incident in the 1950s at Corfe Castle with the stationmaster's cat when a van containing over a hundred milk churns was derailed while coming out of the sidings. 'Hearing a crashing sound, I looked out of the "M7". I saw the van off the track and leaning at an alarming angle. Milk was pouring out of every crack in the van's timber bodywork and forming a huge lake of milk. I'll always remember Mr Chapman's ginger cat sitting quite contentedly licking up the milk — it had never seen so much milk in its whole life.'

Driver Norman missed the last weeks of Swanage branch steam in August and the first four days of September 1966. Instead, he was away learning the new diesel traction for the branch in the future — however short that future was to be.

The 'Hampshire' class three-coach DEMUs and the push-pull-fitted Class 33 diesel-electric locomotives — together with the Class 74 diesel-electrics, as well as the '4TC' non-motor push-pull carriage sets — were to work the branch after the end of steam, until closure took place. BR management hoped that would be the shortest possible period. Fred also trained on the new main line electric REP 'push-pull' stock for the London to Bournemouth line — a world away from what Jack Spicer and Jock Hapgood knew down at Swanage.

During the final years of the branch, the camaraderie and special world of the steam footplate was replaced by the loneliness, boredom and deafening sound of the 'Hampshire' DEMU's diesel-electric engines. 'The "Hampshires" certainly couldn't have coped

Left:
A depressing sight — a decaying Swanage station just three years before it closed. With paint peeling, the run-round loop and bay tracks long gone and the ever-present threat that the train service could be withdrawn at any time, the 600hp engine of grimy three-coach 'Hampshire' DEMU, No 1128, idles impatiently as it waits to form the 13.48 train to Corfe Castle and Wareham on Saturday 23 August 1969. *John H. Bird*

Bottom left:
After four years of disuse and deterioration — and with the threat of demolition finally lifted — Swanage Railway Society volunteers began the long, hard job of restoring the Victorian station and its long rusting canopy in 1976. With the platform bulldozed, running a train seemed a long way off — even to the most ardent and committed enthusiast. *Peter Sykes*

Bottom right:
Passengers would be forgiven for thinking that the Swanage Railway was never taken up. After arriving with the last tain of the day from Harman's Cross, ex-Midland Railway '1F' 0-6-0T No 41708 of 1880 basks in the evening sunshine under Swanage station's restored 1938 canopy on Saturday 6 July 1991. *Andrew P. M. Wright*

with the snows like the old "M7s",' says Fred with a quiet smile. But, when running down the bank from Furzebrook to Worgret or Harman's Cross to Swanage, they would run very fast indeed.'

Fred Norman worked the branch for the last time on the dull afternoon of 1 January 1972, before being relieved by Johnny Walker at Wareham, when a second 'Hampshire' DEMU joined the first for the final trip down to Swanage.

'Johnny was a real gentleman and a very good driver with a wealth of experience. It was sad to see him drive the last train out of Swanage that night — the end of an era and a way of life.'

'I never thought the line would come back because of the way that BR and local authorities were then being pushed by politicians and the road lobby. BR Network SouthEast's attitude to the Swanage Railway in the late 1980s and 1990s couldn't be better.

'Back in 1972, BR management was forced to follow the orders of Government and the Department of Transport. They didn't have any choice in the matter.

'I have been amazed at what the Swanage Railway volunteers have been able to achieve — and I'm not ashamed to admit it. I may have sometimes winced at the way they have done things but who am I to tell them. The history books and future generations will judge them.'

The Main Line Driver's Tale

7

'Climbing up on to the footplate after 23 years, it all suddenly came back to me — like putting on a well-worn, favourite glove. It was so comfortable, so relaxing, so right.'

Stan Symes

As veteran driver Stan Symes speeds through the Hampshire countryside at the controls of his final 12-coach London to Bournemouth express train one late September afternoon, he wonders how best to break some bad news.

Leaving the grimy REP's familiar cab for the final time on the last day of September 1987 — and later handing in his dog-eared books and keys to the train crew supervisor — he ended a career that had spanned 48 years, one and a half million miles and over 90 different forms of traction. It was also to be the end of his seven-year involvement with the enthusiastic volunteers of the Swanage Railway as their teacher of locomotive rules and practice — or so he thought.

Stan was determined to sever his links with the Purbeck Line. He had now retired from British Rail and did not really want to keep on going down to the Swanage Railway or continue taking the Mutual Improvement Classes for their operations volunteers at Bournemouth station.

However, Stan Symes was blissfully unaware that the Swanage Railway volunteers were waiting at the station with a special and touching presentation as a token of their

thanks to him and his wife, Joan, for all their help. 'I just didn't have the courage or the heart to tell them. My resolve just evaporated there and then — and here I am still with the Swanage Railway five years later,' remembers Stan with a smile.

Stan has good reason to remember the old Swanage branch line with nostalgic affection, because he regularly worked on it from the early 1940s until 1969, when the last through-train ran from London down to Swanage in October of that year. Stan has fired and driven push-pull trains, goods and through-trains down to the Purbecks in the 1940s; drove goods and clay trains in the 1950s, Bulleid Pacifics in the 1960s and finally the 'turn of a key' Class 33 diesel-electric locomotives with their '4TC' 'push-pull' sets as the swinging 1960s came to an end.

'I drove my very first train on my own from Bournemouth down to Swanage in the late 1940s,' remembers Stan as he looks back on his long railway career which began back in August 1939 — just days before the outbreak of World War 2.

Stan Symes first walked apprehensively into Bournemouth shed at 6am on Monday 28 August 1939. He was joining a team of 40 cleaners. The following Sunday, the country and the Southern Railway were at war against Nazi Germany. The first two engines he cleaned on that first morning were 'King Arthur' class locomotive No 789 and then 'Schools' class engine No 926 *Repton*. Nearly 30 years later, *Repton* was sold to a United States millionaire and exported to the Steamtown exhibition centre in 1967. She returned to Britain from Pennsylvania, together with ex-Swanage branch 'M7' No 30053, in 1987.

After starting as a temporary cleaner for twenty-four shillings a week, Stan stepped on to the footplate of an engine and first experienced the world of the fireman on Christmas Eve 1939.

'People earn more now in an hour than I did then in a whole week. As a cleaner, if I was borrowed to do a firing turn then I'd be paid

Below:
BBC TV producer/researcher Joe Godwin and his film crew listen intently as Stan Symes talks about his 48-year career with the Southern Railway and British Rail at Swanage station on Sunday 14 March 1988. The *Backtracking on Beeching?* programme examined the revival of railways, and the new spirit of co-operation between BR and the Swanage Railway. *Andrew P. M. Wright*

an extra nine shillings a day. Each year I progressed up the grades and after six years I was on the top grade and the full rate of pay.'

Starting to fire steam locomotives in 1940, Stan stopped being a cleaner and became a full fireman in March 1943. He was a main line fireman and passed driver from 1949 before becoming a fully-fledged driver on the London main line in 1957. In 1943, Stan was taking home 54 shillings a day together with an extra half a crown cost-of-living bonus. By 1953, when a main line fireman, he was earning two extra days' pay including mileage allowances, which came to nine pounds and ten shillings. In 1957, main line drivers were taking home £14.

'That was the big thing about the railways then — companionship between the driver and firemen, who worked together as a tightly-knit team. That was what made the job and something that was sadly missing on the railways when I retired. Drivers and firemen were each reliant on the other.

'The late George Frampton really taught me how to fire a steam locomotive and coax the best out of it. I owe him so much — I was really lucky as a young cleaner to get him because George was excellent. We regularly worked together on the push-and-pull gang at Bournemouth and used to work down to Swanage on our regular "M7" tank. We became firm friends despite the age gap. I must have been 18 and he in his mid-40s but that didn't seem to matter.'

Stan can remember servicing the two rail-mounted guns during World War 2 that were stabled in short sidings near the Motala Kennels at Norden.

The Westinghouse compressed air system on the 'M7' enabled the driver to control the regulator from his cab at the far end of the train via a brass cranked handle. 'I liked push-pull work on the branch because there was plenty of time between trains. The fireman was, more often than not, in complete control of the footplate, when the driver was at the other end of the train, so you had a greater feeling of responsibility and therefore job satisfaction.

'We'd work down from Bournemouth to Swanage, then run empty train back up to Wareham before working a train from there back to Poole and Bournemouth for the workers at the Royal Naval Cordite Factory at Holton Heath. One of my regular mates was driver Deary, who had a terrible stutter.'

Stan remembers one incident at Corfe Castle during World War 2 when a mix-up nearly left his driver standing as the push-pull train accelerated away from him — with Stan still on the footplate of the 'M7'.

'I heard the bell, replied and started off past the "up" starter signal, out of the loop and into the Challow Hill cutting through the Purbeck Hills. All of a sudden, the brake went on and we came to a shuddering halt. I wondered what was going on, pushed the blackout curtain aside and looked out of the "M7" and down the train. The driver was running back alongside the train to me.

'Then, the regulator suddenly flew open and the train lurched forward, leaving him standing on the trackside. We didn't have guards on the push-pull trains then. I quickly closed the regulator and applied the brake on the "M7".

'It turned out the driver didn't put the brake on — he only thought he did. He'd probably touched the brake and, instead of pressing the bell, had inadvertently left the

Above left:
With driver Bob Mitchell leaning out of the cab to collect the single-line tablet in its pouch from the signalman, 'M7' 0-4-4T No 30111 accelerates out of Swanage station with a train for Corfe Castle and Wareham in March 1956. In tow is a two-coach LSWR 'push-pull' set of a type that ran on the branch until the late 1950s. No 30111 was known for her free-steaming and gained the nick-name 'Lord Nelson' in her early years. Built in 1904, she was withdrawn from Bournemouth MPD in May 1964.
Dr Gerald Siviour

Above:
A sight so familiar at Swanage from 1946 until 1967. Newly-restored 120-ton bulk of unrebuilt 'Battle of Britain' class Bulleid Pacific No 34072 *257 Squadron* simmers at Swanage station before departing with the 14.30 train to Harman's Cross on Saturday 30 March 1991. Built in 1948, No 34072 was withdrawn in 1964 and consigned to the Barry scrapyard in South Wales. Restored in a record time of under two years at Tarmac's Swindon Heritage Centre, *257 Squadron* was welcomed to the Swanage Railway in November 1990 by wartime members of the World War 2 RAF squadron. *Andrew P. M. Wright*

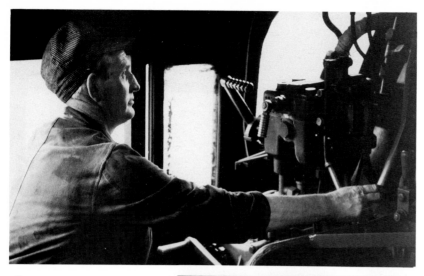

Above:
Driver Stan Symes of Bournemouth MPD at the controls of a 'West Country' class Bulleid Pacific at Swanage in the summer of 1966 as it departs with a through train for London Waterloo during the final summer of branch steam traction. During his 48-year career with the Southern Railway and then BR, Stan drove over one-and-a-half million miles; the equivalent of 62 times round the world or six times to the moon!
Chris Phillips

Above right:
Stan Symes sits at the controls of a Bulleid Pacific at Swanage station for the first time since 1966. With Stan on the footplate of newly restored 'Battle of Britain' class Bulleid Pacific No 34072 *257 Squadron* during her welcoming ceremony on Saturday 10 November 1990, is Harry Frith, ex-erecting shop foreman of BR's huge Eastleigh works which built and maintained the Bulleid Pacific locomotives from the 1940s through to 1967.
Andrew P. M. Wright

the signalman let us run into the coal dock road. It was raining and as we ran in my driver, Fred Smith, put on the brake as we reached the coal dock to take water. We didn't stop. Instead, we slid on the wet, greasy rails across the turntable and hit the corner of the engine shed, which then had doors. The collision had cracked the crown of the arch and there was a huge crack up the entire side of the wall.'

Becoming a passed fireman, Stan Symes drove his first train from Bournemouth down to Corfe Castle and Swanage during the summer of 1949. He and his fireman relieved a 'Merchant Navy' and took the 10-coach London excursion train on from there. The locomotive was Maunsell 'Q' class 0-6-0 No 30541. Twenty-five years later in 1974, she was rescued from Barry Scrapyard in 1974, fully restored by the Maunsell Locomotive Society and is now running on the Bluebell Railway in Sussex.

'I had driven before, but with a driver with me and taking it in turns with him. This was the first time that I was on the footplate with just a fireman Stan Ierson — and 10 coaches filled with people behind that were my responsibility. Being in command was a very different feeling.

'I was nervous as I climbed on to the footplate of No 30541 at Bournemouth, I do remember that. It wasn't fright — that's too strong a word for it — but I was anxious about getting it all right. It was also a heavy train with tight timings for getting to Poole, Wareham and then Swanage, so that made me even more concerned at doing the job properly.

'I was really knocking her about as we ran down to Branksome, Parkstone and Poole. Then, I realised that my regular driver — Frank Carter — wouldn't be rushing around and treating the locomotive the way I was. As soon as I remembered how he would have done the job, it had a calming effect and I relaxed.

'Frank was a wonderful man and my regular driver on "Merchant Navy" class Bulleid Pacific No 35027 *Port Line* at Bournemouth. Although he had no mechanical knowledge, Frank had a sixth sense about driving a steam locomotive. He was remarkable, I've never learnt so much from one man.'

regulator open. He thought I'd stopped the train. As he got down from his cab, walked the length of two coaches to the "M7", the vacuum had been recreated and — with the regulator open — off the train shot.'

In another incident Stan remembers well, a signalman's error at Bournemouth caused an 'M7' to over-shoot the turntable over at Swanage station one rainy day and career into the engine shed — causing significant damage.

'By 1943, I was on the push-and-pull gang at Bournemouth — known as the "Tug-and-Shove". My first driver was Fred Smith and then George Frampton after that. We also had our own engines, which we kept clean. We'd take a train from Bournemouth to Wareham and then back along the main line to Christchurch before working back to Bournemouth.

'On one occasion, we took on coal and water at Bournemouth, ready to depart for Swanage. But, due to a signalling error, we couldn't run round the train and so had to pull it bunker-first down to Corfe Castle and Swanage instead of pushing it.

'When we reached Swanage, of course, the "M7" was on the wrong end of the train and had to run round the train. That we did but

With the end of Southern Region steam on the morning of Monday 10 July 1967, Stan transferred off the sooty and grubby Bulleid Pacifics, Standard and Ivatt tanks, into a new, clean driver's uniform — and then into the cabs of the new 'REP' electric units and the Class 33 diesel-electric diesels. But the end of

Left:
Branch and main line trains meet at Wareham station on a summer morning in 1966. Ex-LMS Ivatt 2-6-2T No 41224 waits patiently with the 11.28 to Corfe Castle and Swanage in the south bay platform 1 on Saturday 21 May 1966. The 1949-built 'Merchant Navy' class Bulleid Pacific No 35030 *Elder Dempster Lines* drifts in with the 08.30 Waterloo to Weymouth train. *John Scrace*

Centre left:
Just five months later, steam traction to Swanage had gone and main line steam on the Southern Region of BR only had 11 months to live. The first day of branch diesel operation on Monday 5 September 1966, the 600hp diesel engine of three-coach 'Hampshire' DEMU, No 1104, idles noisily with the 15.44 to Corfe and Swanage, as BR Standard class 5 4-6-0 No 73113 trundles past with the 15.01 Bournemouth Central to Weymouth stopping train. *John H. Bird*

Below:
Sporting the red, white and blue logo of BR Network SouthEast, four-coach '4-Cig' class electric train No 1307 stands at Wareham station's 'down' platform on Saturday 6 July 1991, with a morning stopping train to Bournemouth, Southampton and Portsmouth. The old bay for Swanage trains has become a car park. Fully diesel-operated from Monday 10 July 1967, the main line through Wareham was electrified and the station fully restored in 1988 when the new Class 442 'Wessex Electric' trains were introduced.
Andrew P. M. Wright

steam and the 'Battle of Britain' and 'West Country' Pacifics did not mean the end of his visits to Corfe Castle and Swanage. 'I still came down the branch with London trains after the summer of 1966. Then, of course, they were made up of 4TC non-motor stock and hauled by either a Class 33 diesel-electric or a Class 74 electro-diesel. But it was sad to work into Swanage during the summer of 1967 with only the main line in use, the signalbox closed and with the rest of the station tracks waiting to be lifted.

'After the track to Corfe and Swanage was lifted, I didn't think the railway volunteers of the Swanage Railway Society could ever bring it back. And when they did start with a few sleepers and rails I have to admit that I thought they were just playing trains.

'It wasn't until I started taking the Mutual Improvement Classes for the Swanage Railway staff at Bournemouth station in 1981 — and saw the sheer determination of the volunteers to succeed in their aims — that I realised how wrong I'd been. I completely changed my opinion overnight. The first time I went down to the railway, saw what they'd achieved

and how friendly and amiable they were, I had to admit I'd been wrong.'

Stan's colleagues back at Bournemouth could not understand why a man who had been in the top driving link for over 30 years, driven on Canadian railways, worked on over 90 different forms of traction — and notched up an astounding one-and-a-half million miles during his career — should want to drive what

Above:

On a warm summer day in 1961, an eight-coach through train from London Waterloo disturbs the rural peace as it winds its way through the Afflington cutting en route from Corfe Castle to Swanage — carrying nearly 500 excited holidaymakers from the hustle and bustle of the capital to the peace of the sea. A common occurrence, the train is double-headed by rebuilt 'West Country' class Bulleid Pacific No 34093 *Saunton* of 1949 and 'M7' 0-4-4T No 30107 built in 1905.
Mike Esau

Above right:

Slowly, the railway returns to Corfe Castle. On a misty morning, ex-BR Class 08 diesel shunter No D3591 of 1958, steadily pushes the Swanage Railway's track-relaying train through the Afflington cutting, heading for Corfe Castle on Friday 13 April 1990. The ex-Southern Railway 15-ton diesel-electric crane prepares to lay another 60ft track panel. Just a few weeks before, this view was completely blocked by thick undergrowth and trees that had grown up in the 18 years since the old BR track was lifted.
Andrew P. M. Wright

they considered to be 'toy' trains on a tiny one-and-a-half mile line at Swanage.

'They thought I was playing trains. I told them they didn't know what they were talking about and why didn't they come down to Swanage and try it for themselves? But, none of them had the courage to do it,' remembers Stan with smile. 'Some thought I was nuts to do it — and I'm sure some of my ex-colleagues still do.'

However, Stan stuck to his guns and in November 1990 received his reward when he drove the first Bulleid Pacific to leave Swanage station since June 1967. The history-making occasion saw Stan at the controls of unrebuilt 'Battle of Britain' class Bulleid Pacific No 34072 *257 Squadron*, as she ran up to Harman's Cross for the first time with a six-coach train.

'She handled very well apart from a couple of half-slips when leaving Swanage because of

the rain. It must have been over 23 years since I last climbed on a Bulleid Pacific but, looking at the controls of *257 Squadron*, it was as though I'd never been away.'

A delighted Stan reached an important milestone in December 1991, when he worked on his 100th class of locomotive since he started his railway career back in 1939. The piece of history was not made on British Rail, but the Swanage Railway's Purbeck Line. 'J72' class 0-6-0T No 69023 *Joem* was the lucky locomotive — build for BR in 1951 and on loan from the North Eastern Locomotive Preservation Group who normally run her on the 18-mile North York Moors Railway — and the occasion, a Swanage to Harman's Cross 'Santa Special' steam train carrying 400 equally excited children and parents.

More memories were to be stirred at Swanage. In the spring of 1991 Stan was able to renew his long-time acquaintance with the

Left:
Victorian 'M7' 0-4-4T No 30111 clatters down the 1 in 80 gradient past Corfe Common and the station's distant signal with a mid-day train for Corfe Castle and Wareham on Saturday 19 August 1961. The train is made up of a single ex-Southern Railway strengthening coach normally kept by the stopblocks at Swanage, and a two-coach 'Ironclad' 'push-pull' set.
Mike Esau

Dugald Drummond designed 'T9' 'Greyhound' 4-4-0 No 30120. When Stan clambered up on to her Victorian footplate to drive her the three miles up to Harman's Cross, it was the first time that he had driven a 'T9' since the early 1960s.

'Climbing on board, it all suddenly came back — like putting on a well-worn, favourite glove. It was so comfortable, so relaxing, so right. If anyone had told me then that I would not miss a job that I spent nearly 50 years doing, I would have laughed in his face. But, I don't miss it at all — and the Swanage Railway suits me perfectly.'

Below left:
The same scene looking across Corfe Common towards the Afflington cutting in April 1989, with the top cut off the rusting LSWR lattice distant signal post and gorse bushes and trees choking the trackbed. The track through here was lifted by Eagre & Co of Scunthorpe during the final week of July, 1972.
Andrew P. M. Wright

Bottom left:
Stan Symes is rendered almost speechless by a surprise presentation by fellow Swanage Railway volunteers on Saturday 7 December 1991. When he worked on his 100th different class of steam engine. 'I wasn't expecting anything like this — how did you keep it all a secret?' asks Stan as he faces a sea of beaming faces belonging to his fellow drivers, firemen and cleaners — and a local ITV camera crew from the Television South 'Coast to Coast' news programme. With Stan are Swanage Railway Co Chairman David Cash and Margaret Clarke — an early Swanage Railway volunteer from the early 1970s.
Andrew P. M. Wright

The Signalman's Tale

'The brake van was still standing out on the main line at Furzebrook. We couldn't believe it but there was nothing we could do. The 15.37 to Swanage was speeding down from Worgret Junction — heading for a collision.'

Jimmy Hunt

Had it not been for the quiet words of wisdom from his father, 20-year-old Jimmy Hunt would not have stuck it as a temporary summer porter on Swanage station in March 1949.

Nearly 20 years later, Jimmy stands on Northbrook Bridge one day in November 1967, looking down at the skeletal remains of Swanage station with just one track leading to the main platform. Contractors are busy lifting all the other tracks and cutting up the old turntable outside the engine shed. There is a nauseous, acrid smell in the air as the scrapmen's oxy-acetylene torches burn into the rails and oily sleepers. A bulldozer determinedly lays into the old LSWR signalbox, which closed the previous summer. The cracking sound of splintering and breaking wood, glass and metal echoes in Jimmy's ears.

The previous March, he had worked his last shift in that signalbox, putting his cloth over one of the levers and locking the green door before skipping down the worn steps to his car for the last time.

Faces and voices of the railwaymen he worked with over the years come flooding back as Jimmy stands on the windswept bridge; Harry Galton and his son Arthur, little Ted Morley and Ray Anstey, Arthur Mee-

han, Frank Kitcatt and Bob Inman. His memories of times past are shattered as the dull sound of metal striking metal hits Jimmy's ears. Two workmen with heavy lump hammers pound the old lever frame — smashing it into pieces. Jimmy recalls the hours he spent keeping the frame sparkling clean. Every blow hurts as it echoes around the desolate station. A few feet away from the remains of the box, acrid blue smoke drifts up from a huge bonfire, before being swirled away by the easterly wind. Old relics from the box — faded track and signalling diagrams, dusty papers hoarded from half a century before as well as the old linoleum floor, wooden panelling and window frames — are all quickly consumed by the ravenous fire.

Jimmy Hunt's railway career started nearly 20 years before. Fresh from two years National Service, which he admits that he enjoyed, Jimmy found himself at home in Swanage in March 1949 — and homesick for the mates he left back in the Army. He was persuaded to join the railway while he decided his future, but in the end, the branch line was to decide it for him.

'On my first day at Swanage as a summer porter, I reported to the station foreman, Bill

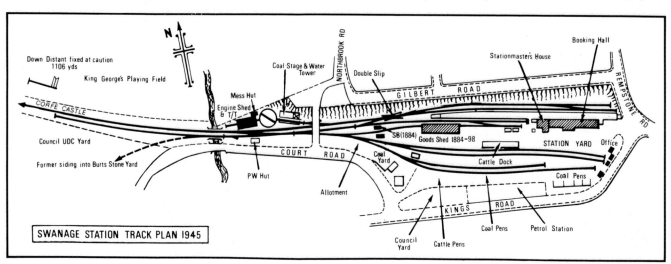

SWANAGE STATION TRACK PLAN 1945

Facing page, top:
Swanage signalman Jimmy Hunt turns up for work at Swanage station one morning in March 1965 on his highly-prized red Vesper scooter.
Chris Phillips

Facing page, bottom:
Twenty-six years later, Jimmy Hunt returns to Corfe Castle station's 'up' platform on Saturday 1 June 1991. Standing by the post-1956 signalbox — an extension to the porter's lobby — Jimmy simulates the exchange of the single-line key-token in its loop pouch; something he did thousands of times during his career with British Rail. It could be a tricky manoeuvre if the locomotive was running light through the station at speed and the crew keen to get back to Bournemouth depot! *Andrew P. M. Wright*

Above left:
Swanage station's 1884 Victorian LSWR signalbox basks in the sunshine one summer evening in 1964 and viewed from the Gilbert Road with the town behind. Next to the box, signalman Arthur Galton can be seen by his car. After closure on Tuesday 6 June 1967, the box was demolished in November 1967, with its 26-lever frame being sold to Channel Metals of Poole. Swanage's last signalman — Arthur Galton — was transferred to Corfe Castle where he worked with Bob Richards until the branch line closed. *John Lakey*

Left:
The interior of Swanage signalbox showing the 23-lever frame between steam trains from Corfe Castle one summer afternoon in 1966. In the far corner is the Tyers No 6 single-line tablet machine for the section of line to Corfe Castle. 'I liked working at Swanage', remembers Jimmy Hunt, 'because there was more to keep your mind occupied. But, it could be boiling in the summer and freezing in the winter', muses Jimmy nearly 25 years after the box was demolished. *Chris Phillips*

James, at 8am sharp. He was one of the old type of railwaymen. My first uniform was splendid with its green lapels, shining Southern Railway buttons and badges on the collar. It was a nice uniform and I felt proud when I put it on.

'But, the money was better — four pounds twelve shillings and sixpence as compared with two pounds and twelve shillings in the Army. My railway wage went up to seven pounds and two shillings in 1957 when I got married. By the time I left British Rail in March 1967, I was only on £11 or £12.

'Bill James taught me how to shunt. Bill couldn't run so fast and we'd be shunting 10 to 12 wagons in the headshunt opposite the engine shed at Swanage and letting them roll back into whichever sidings we wanted them

to end up in. The idea was for Bill to run alongside the wagons and apply the brakes with his shunting pole, but often he couldn't catch up with the wagons. One day, Bill was running past the wagons with his shunting pole when he tripped over and the wagons went hurtling into the goods shed doors. There was hell to pay over that.'

But, as well as learning the mysteries of shunting — and how to cut corners — Jimmy did not ingratiate himself with the station staff when he spent his first week working in the goods shed.

'I was helping Bill Laird, the goods checker, and George Symes, the temporary goods porter, to unload boxes of champagne for the prestigious Grosvenor Hotel in Swanage. While helping to unload them out of the box van and on to the railway lorry, I tripped, dropped a box — loudly smashing all the bottles. Mr Bannister gave me a good telling off and told me to be more careful.'

Jimmy Hunt's first job as a porter/signalman in 1950 was the midday relief in Swanage box, replacing Albert Smith, who had moved to Corfe where he worked the booking office.

'I'd fill in between 12 noon and 3pm between the early and late turns and do one of the two shifts if the signalman was off ill or on holiday. My little black terrier dog "Trumps" loved it in the signalbox. He used to sit on the steps watching the engines shunting up and down the line.

'If I was late getting home, he'd trot down to the station and I'd hear him scratching at the door and see his two little eyes peering through the glass. But, he didn't like everyone and used to attack poor old Eddy Bird, who was on the track gang at Swanage.

'Then I was working with Ray Anstey and Ted Morley. Ted was a funny character — quite a thin and weedy little man of a very nervous disposition who had a very amorous wife. She used to come into the box when he was on duty and fling herself on him and then have a kiss and a cuddle in the corner.'

Jimmy remembers one humorous incident when a forgetful signalman caused a panic not only at Corfe Castle signalbox but at the Southern Region district control at Southampton — giving Ted Morley the fright of his life. 'Ray Anstey was working the late turn in Swanage box and Jim Lightbody was at Corfe Castle. After driver Jack Spicer

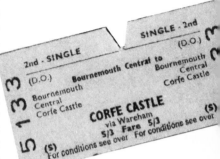

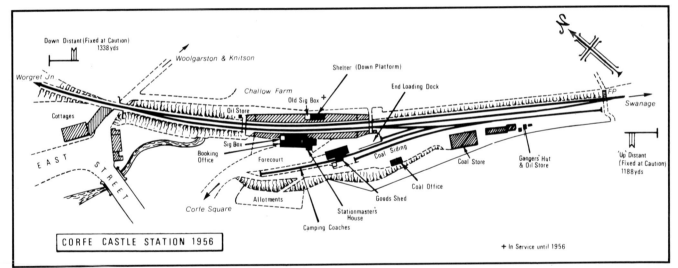

CORFE CASTLE STATION 1956

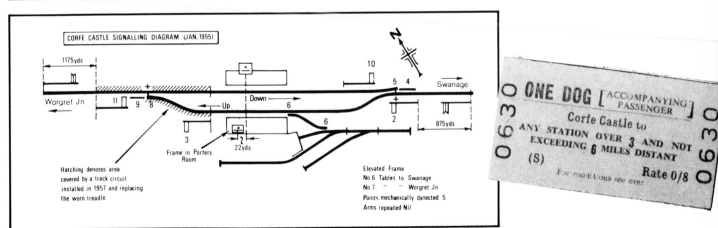

worked the last train down to Swanage, the locomotive ran round its carriages before Ray signalled it into the coal dock road. He then closed the signalbox and went home.

'Ray had forgotten to close signals with Corfe Castle, where Jim Lightbody was still waiting for the out of section signal from Swanage, so he could put his single-line tablet away.

'When the control office at Southampton got through to Jack, they were told that Ray had gone home. Jack was despatched to retrieve Ray. But, Jack couldn't find his house, so control phoned the police station in Swanage. It was the early hours by now and poor old Jim Lightbody was still waiting to put his tablet away, close up the signalbox and go home.

'Control got through to Bill Aplin at the police station, who asked him to fetch poor old Ted Morley out of bed. Ted was due to be the early turn signalman at Swanage the following morning.

'Hearing the door, Ted came down to answer it in his pyjamas. Opening it, he saw the burly figure of Police Officer Aplin standing there. Bill asked him to come down to the station but poor old Ted fainted on the spot, forcing the policeman to take the signalman unconscious back up to bed. Ted had thought Bill meant the police station — not the railway station!

'There was hell to pay over that incident,' says Jimmy laughing. 'It was serious then, but seems too ridiculous now. Ray got three days'

suspension without pay from Mr Bannister, the stationmaster, and poor old Ted Morley had several days sick because of the shock of it all.'

In the summer months Jimmy had to get to Corfe for 5.30am on his treasured Lambretta scooter to accept the early morning paper train from Wareham. In 1960, he was nearly killed after coming off his scooter on black ice early one morning while travelling to Corfe. Putting duty first — and realising the paper train would soon be approaching Worgret Junction — he hitched a lift to Corfe Castle, his head bleeding profusely. Jimmy's only regret after the accident was that he only received £20 for the scrap value of his prized scooter!

'My wife Heidi and my baby daughter, Caroline, used to visit me when I was on duty at Corfe Castle. Between trains we used to go and sit on East Hill, which overlooked the railway. From up there it looked for the world like a model railway.

'The public, especially children, used to trespass through the wire fence and on to the line near the cutting into East Hill as a short cut. I used to pull the Wareham-end point of Corfe loop suddenly shut, so the crack of the blades would frighten them off.'

Most railwaymen — like Jimmy — were forced to moonlight outside railway hours to boost their income. Fellow signalman Bob

Inman used to make picture frames for sixpence a time in the small garden next to Corfe Castle signalbox between trains. He also made his greenhouse there as well.

'I used to do taxi driving around Swanage as well as gardening, which paid three shillings an hour in 1957, remembers Jimmy. 'That later went up to four shillings a hour and augmented my railway wage of around £12 a week — and that's including overtime. Fellow signalman, Ray Anstey, put me on to that.'

On another occasion, a panicking branch driver — who feared he had lost the single-line tablet — caused chaos on the branch, when the usual 10 minute journey time between Swanage and Corfe Castle took half an hour.

'Jack Spicer used to be a worrier. He was working a push-pull train from Swanage to Corfe Castle one afternoon when he thought he'd lost the pouch with the single-line tablet in it.

'Jack searched for it as the train approached Corfe but couldn't find it. He was so embarrassed at the thought of being found that out he stopped his train out just of sight of Corfe station, had one more try at finding it before driving back to Swanage.

'By this time, of course, the "down" train was waiting at Corfe for the Swanage train to arrive. Bob Inman, the Corfe signalman was wondering where on earth the Swanage train had got to. He called me at Swanage. I told Bob that the train had left 10 minutes before. We just couldn't think where poor old Jack had got to. Had he had an accident?

'Reaching the approaches to Swanage — but out of sight of the station — he again frantically searched the "M7's" footplate and the driving compartment of the carriage set with his fireman. Still not being able to find the tablet he stayed there wondering what to do. Should he go into Swanage and tell the signalman — and be the laughing stock of the station — or should he go back to Corfe in the hope of finding it before getting there, he thought.

'The passengers were leaning out of the train wondering what was going on as they ran back and forth between Corfe and Swanage. After a few minutes of thinking it over, he continued back to Corfe but still couldn't find it. Then, as he ran down the straight into the station he found it! But, by then, the train had taken nearly half an hour to travel the five miles.'

There was another incident which prompted a desperate cover-up by the staff concerned after an experienced guard's absent-mindedness nearly caused a crash at Furzebrook clay sidings.

'Harvey Day at Worgret Junction gave me the signal asking if the line to Corfe Castle was clear for the 3.37pm passenger train to proceed. I signalled it was with the appropriate bell code and held my plunger in so Harvey could then draw a tablet and give it to the driver of the Swanage-bound train.

'But, the worst had happened. I was waiting for the train to arrive at Corfe when the phone rang in the box. It was guard Alec Dudley. He said his train was locked in the loop at Furzebrook — but that he'd forgotten to include the brake van after shunting the wagons. It was still standing out on the main line. We couldn't believe it but there was nothing we could do. The 3.37pm was speeding down from Worgret Junction, heading for a collision with the brake van. Luckily, the train crew was keeping a lookout and saw the van and Alec frantically waving his red flag as they climbed the gradient to the sidings. The train was able to stop in good time.

'Once the passenger train came to a halt, Harvey and I were forced to communicate with each other via bell codes only, so that no-one else on the railway found out what was going on. It broke every rule in the railway rule book.

'The best part of my career was spent in Swanage signalbox, because I respond to pressure and responsibility — and on a hectic summer Saturday there was a lot of that. You had to be on the ball in making sure that you could accept trains, signal them in, allow them to do their work and then find a path for them to leave again without throwing the timetable into chaos. That's why quite a few trains were double-headed, so you could return two engines in one 'path' to Wareham and Bournemouth.'

Working the 23-lever frame at Swanage did have its disadvantages, especially where lever No 2 was concerned. 'That lever operated the "down" home signal at Swanage, which was quite a way from the box. You needed a lot of muscle and really had to put your full body weight behind it to pull the lever over. Once, the signal cable broke, flinging me back across the box and into the log book table. Another problem lever was No 6.'

Despite being on the Swanage branch for 18 years and, by his own admission, loving the work and the railway staff he worked with, Jimmy Hunt decided to leave British Rail in March 1967.

'It wasn't a snap decision,' he remembers. 'I thought about it for a long time. It was an agonising decision. By the time I left, the line

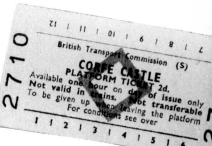

Left:
The last occasion that a steam locomotive ran on the Swanage branch was on the warm summer morning of Friday 30 June 1967. Slotted in between two DEMU trains, rebuilt 'West Country' Bulleid Pacific No 34025 *Whimple* collects the clay wagons from the works of Pike Brothers Fayle & Co at Furzebrook. Shorn of her nameplate and number, the grimy 1946-built locomotive is just eight days from withdrawal.
George M. Moon

Below:
By 1991 Furzebrook had changed yet again, with export of oil from BP's Wytch Farm field switching to propane and butane gas. After the loading terminal was converted in a multi-million pound operation during early 1990, the first gas train ran in October of that year. On the hot morning of Saturday 29 June 1991, BR's new Class 60 diesel-electric locomotive No 60024 *Elizabeth Fry* departs Furzebrook for Avonmouth.
Andrew P. M. Wright

Top right:
The interior of Corfe Castle signalbox showing the 12-lever frame on the Swanage branch's last day of operation, Saturday 1 January 1972. Arthur Galton worked the early turn (05.45-13.45) with Bob Richards doing the late (13.45-23.00) — and becoming the final signalman at the Victorian station on the first day of the branch's 87th year of operation. The last train was the six-coach 22.15 from Swanage which arrived at Corfe at 22.23 and left a minute later for Bournemouth — for the last time.
John H. Bird

Below:
Three veteran Swanage branch signalmen return to their old haunt at Corfe Castle signalbox on Saturday 1 June 1991. From left to right are Jimmy Hunt, Bob Richards and Bob Inman. For Jimmy Hunt and Bob Inman, it was the first time they had set foot in the box since they left BR in March 1967. Bob Richards worked in the box from September 1968, until the last day of operation. Bob Inman made good use of his time at Corfe between trains, making picture frames for sixpence a time, and even his greenhouse, in the small station garden.
Andrew P. M. Wright

was being run with one DEMU set. The station was soon to be rationalised with all the tracks coming out except for the one running line.

'Stationmaster Harry Newman had moved to Brockenhurst with the whole branch now under Bill Langford at Wareham — and staff redundancies at Swanage station were only four months away. Just three months after Bob Inman and I left, the signalbox at Swanage was closed in early June 1967, with Arthur Galton moving to Corfe Castle.

'My last week at Swanage was terrible — I was literally worried sick. I had an upset stomach, couldn't sleep and didn't even want to eat. After all those years on the railway I was nervous as to whether I was doing the right thing — and how I'd cope with a new job "on the outside". The Swanage branch line had been my life since I was 20 years old.

'What really caught in our throats was watching management spending money hand over fist on a branch which they knew was going to close only a year or two later. They put water and electricity into the signalbox, installed new points, track circuits and point rodding only a year or two before the whole lot was ripped out for scrap in 1967.

'Watching the signalbox at Swanage being smashed up and burnt in late 1967 was awful — almost too painful to watch after spending over 15 years working in it. I always wondered what happened to the old signalbox clock, which I had spent thousands of hours looking at. I used to look up at it and think how many generations of signalmen must have done the same over the years.

'The first time I stepped inside that signalbox was back in the summer of 1949. Then it was the preserve of signalman Harry Galton, who seemed very Victorian to a young man of 20 years of age. He told me off for standing on the floor which he'd just polished telling me to sit in the corner and be quiet.

'After seeing it all smashed up I never thought the railway would come back to Swanage — never — and certainly not reach Harman's Cross and Corfe Castle. I know a lot of local people like me, who saw the volunteers playing about with a few sleepers and old rails back in 1976, have been forced to eat our words, although few would admit it.

'The smell of steam, warm lubricating oil and coal dust does bring it all back. Watching the trains run on the Swanage Railway is strange, because now I watch it all from the other side of the fence — and closing my eyes it does seem like a summer Saturday in the 1950s or 1960s.'

The Area Manager's Tale

'There aren't the number of people to make it viable. The Swanage Railway won't be anything more than a tourist attraction — it can't be. That's why it closed in 1972, because it just wasn't being used by the travelling public.'

Harold Ward

Harold Ward peers through the small cab window of the grimy 'Hampshire' unit and out into the darkness as the packed six-coach train hurtles through the chilly January night — the dying hours of New Year's Day 1972, slowly slipping away like sand through his fingers. With its passengers leaning out of every available window, the party atmosphere on board makes it feel more like the first train in Purbeck rather than the last.

The tatty and tired-looking diesel train moans and judders its way up from the Frome valley and clatters over the elegant iron river bridge — the 'Hampshire' unit's throaty growl echoing across the neighbouring fields. The last train to Corfe Castle and Swanage

Above left:
The latest 'turn of a key' diesel power at Swanage station in the summer of 1966. One warm early Sunday evening in July, Brush Type 4 (later Class 47) diesel-electric locomotive No D1686 throbs at the head of the eight-coach 18.12 Sundays-only train to Southampton and Eastleigh. Working through trains down to Corfe and Swanage in 1965 and 1966, the Class 47s later returned to the Isle of Purbeck in the late 1970s on BP's bulk oil trains from Furzebrook to South Wales and Fawley. *Chris Phillips*

Below left:
One of the final steam-hauled trains to London Waterloo waits to depart from Swanage station on Saturday 3 September 1966 — just three days before the change to diesel traction on the branch. Rebuilt 'West Country' Bulleid Pacific No 34004 *Yeovil* of Bournemouth MPD simmers at the end of the station platform with her crew chatting in the sun, as they wait for ex-LMS Ivatt 2-6-2T No 41316 to steam in from Corfe Castle, before leaving with the 11.20 train to London. *Colin L. Caddy*

Right:

The residents of Swanage get used to a new sound — the hiss and simmer of steam being replaced by the electric whine and throaty growl of the faceless 'Hampshire' diesel trains. On the first afternoon of an all-diesel service on Monday 5 September 1966, three-coach 'Hampshire' DEMU No 1104 accelerates out of the main platform at Swanage and past the signalbox with the 16.20 to Corfe Castle and Wareham. Just 14 months after this picture was taken, the LSWR signalbox, signals and sidings would be gone — leaving just one track. *John H. Bird*

Centre right:

This is what the volunteers of the Swanage Railway Society faced when they gained access to the disused and boarded-up station in 1976. It was as though the railway never existed. The spectacle of London expresses departing and long goods trains shunting in the sidings has been replaced by a vast wasteland of weed-infested ballast. In this view taken on Friday 12 September 1975, a lone figure wanders across the silent expanse of gravel. A bus and beach peddle boats are parked where trains once waited to leave for Corfe Castle and Wareham. *George M. Moon*

Bottom right:

A scene that Harold Ward admits he never thought he would see. Swanage Railway volunteers have managed to completely rebuild the infrastructure needed to build and run a railway. On the fine evening of Saturday 6 July 1991, three-coach 'Hastings' class DEMU No 1012 departs Swanage station with the 18.00 train to Harman's Cross. The old station yard now houses the town's health centre and a car park. Built in 1957, No 1012 clocked up more than seven million miles during her 30-year career running between London and Hastings for BR. *Andrew P. M. Wright*

tackles the 1 in 78 gradient under Holme Lane bridge and accelerates through Creech — the train's cab lights illuminating only a few feet of the track ahead, as it flashes by in a blur. Then, rounding the bend, driver Johnny Walker suddenly sees the white glow of arc-lights filling above a crowd of people at Creech Bottom's small gated crossing. With its shrill and distinctive two-tone horn sounding, the two 'Hampshire' units growl past a crowd of young men dressed in wild west cowboy outfits and sporting gun holsters. Members of Dorset's county police give an air of sobriety to the almost party-like proceedings as a cameraman from Southern Television expectantly looks on.

'If all those people had used the line it wouldn't be closing,' says Bournemouth area manager Harold Ward with a smile. The crossing glides by amidst shouts and cheers from the watching public along the lineside.

However, nearly 20 years later, the man responsible for the branch line's closure says he has no regrets. 'The Swanage branch line just didn't pay,' says Bournemouth's ex-area manager Harold Ward who retired from British Rail in 1982 after 45 years with the railways.

'In the economic climate of the time and the amount of subsidy available from the government, we just couldn't justify its retention any longer,' adds Harold who left BR to become the private hire executive for Bournemouth international coach operators, Excelsior.

'You can have anything you want in this world if you are prepared to pay for it and, in the case of the railways, use it,' says the man whose career started with the Southern Railway — proud of the family atmosphere amongst its staff — back in 1937.

Growing up in the Southampton of the 1920s, one childhood memory for Harold is of being taken by his parents down to the beach by the railway at Millbrook and paddling where the huge container terminal is now located. After he left school, 17-year-old Harold Ward had two choices — either join the Ordnance Survey in Southampton or go on to the railways. The King's cartographers lost out and Harold opted to become a management trainee with the Southern Railway at its Southampton district office in September 1937. Southampton was then the centre of a huge district that encompassed three counties — from Basingstoke to Weymouth, Portsmouth to Salisbury.

Had it not been for Adolf Hitler marching into Poland, Harold Ward would have followed a career with the marine customs unit at Southampton — and not become involved with railway management and traffic, which would see him charged with the closure of the Swanage branch line 30 years later.

Before volunteering for service with the Royal Engineers' railway division in November 1940, he was involved in helping to route the hundreds of trains that carried exhausted troops rescued from the Dunkirk disaster away from the southeast of England in late May and early June 1940. 'I was working in the control office in Basingstoke during the evacuation. Everywhere you looked there were trains following each other — and coming through so fast and frequently that ordinary signalling was dispensed with. Drivers were told to just look out for the train in front.'

Joining the Royal Engineers, Harold was to spend the next six years running railways both in Britain and war-torn Europe. Landing at Calais in July 1944, after the D-Day Allied landings, he helped to rebuild the railways and run both military and civilian traffic on some of France and Germany's shattered railways that had been destroyed by fierce RAF and the USAAF bombing just weeks before. By 1946, when he was demobbed, the 26-year-old Warrant Officer was in charge of a training centre on the Royal Engineers' Longmoor Military Railway in Hampshire.

Back in civilian life, Harold returned to the Southern Railway at the bottom of the ladder in the flood of demobbed servicemen entering civvy street. He tried to find his 'niche' as the newly-elected Labour government prepared to keep its election promise and nationalise the big four railway companies.

'We were very hopeful about nationalisation. During the war years the railways had been pounded to death, bombed and run on a shoestring. With the coming of peace they were still being run on a shoestring with old stock and Victorian locomotives. People saw nationalisation as the salvation of the industry, because of the prospect of reinvestment, modernisation and change.

'But, nationalisation in 1948 should have included road transport such as coaches and buses as well, so the country had an integrated transport network — as on the continent.'

During his first year back with the Southern Railway, Harold Ward worked on the relief throughout the Southampton district, including frequent visits to the Swanage branch.

'Swanage was a funny old branch,' he remembers. 'It was busy in the summer and then all of a sudden in early October the traffic would drop like a stone and there would be hardly anything apart from the two school trains, the workers' train and a few shoppers. There was also the freight, the clay and the stone traffic.

Out with the old and in with the new. In June 1966, passengers were told that their train service was to be improved. Dirty steam traction was to be scrapped in favour of new, 'clean' diesel-electric multiple-units (DEMUs). But, rather than improving the service, the change was to lead to decline and final closure of the line just five years later. From Monday 5 September 1966, the branch was worked by a single three-coach 'Hampshire' DEMU. Stabled at Bournemouth West carriage sidings, the unit had to return to Eastleigh once a week to be refuelled.
Tim Stephens

Centre right:
Three-coach 'Hampshire' DEMU No 1127 noisily accelerates out of Swanage station and past the recently closed signalbox on Monday 26 June 1967, with a morning train to Corfe Castle and Wareham. The last BR steam train ran down to Swanage just eight days before. Signals have been stripped of their red arms and oil lamps. The rusting bay track and main platform run-round loop lie unused and weed-ridden, not having been used since the previous September.
Swanage's LSWR signalbox closed on Tuesday 6 June 1967, from when the five-mile section from Corfe Castle was worked as a 'long-siding' without signalling. *George M. Moon*

Bottom right:
The new 'streamlined' BR image at Swanage just five years later in 1971 and looking from the end of the main platform towards the Northbrook Road bridge. After ruthless rationalisation in November 1967, just one track remains. The signals, signalbox and all other sidings, run-round loops and headshunts have been torn up. Just the derelict air-raid shelter remains.
Gerry Andrews

84

REVISED TRAIN SERVICE
SWANAGE BRANCH LINE

From MONDAY, 5 SEPTEMBER, the existing weekday steam services between WAREHAM and SWANAGE will be withdrawn and replaced by a modern diesel electric multiple unit service.

Please ask at this station for leaflet giving train timings.

British Rail | Southern Region

'It was this inconsistency that brought about the branch's downfall. Despite what people say and the sentiments expressed, the summer months of traffic alone couldn't justify its retention. It always amused me when I went to meetings over the closure of the Swanage line and asked how many people came to the meeting by train. Only a few put their hands up. When you looked at the facts and figures, the Swanage branch just didn't pay.'

Harold Ward spent the 1950s as the Southampton district's chief commercial representative charged with marketing the railways in Dorset, Hampshire and Wiltshire to industry and commerce in the face of increasingly fierce road competition. Then, in the early 1960s, Harold Ward was appointed to British Railways' infamous Southern Region branch line committee. Their brief was to cost lines such as the Swanage branch, the much-loved Somerset & Dorset main line, the Old Road to Ringwood and Brockenhurst and the cross-country route from West Moors to Salisbury.

Censuses of passengers were taken and detailed service costs logged and analysed, and reports made to the General Manager at Waterloo. It was the figures compiled by Mr Ward and his colleagues that provided the ammunition, the raw material and the *raison d'être* — for Beeching's infamous report on the state of the railways and their future, which was published on Wednesday 27 March 1963.

'For staff and management alike, the Beeching Report was like a bucket of cold water being thrown over us. But, there was a lot of common sense behind the report. Road competition was having its effect. Services such as those on the "Old Road" to Ringwood and Brockenhurst and up to Salisbury just weren't being used enough. Six people on a train couldn't pay for the all-year-round service that we were offering then.

'My criticism of the Beeching Report would be that it didn't go far enough in integrating road and rail transport. It's all very well closing the Swanage branch and saying a bus service will replace the trains when you know that after a time the bus operator will pull out, because it isn't economic.'

In an effort to improve financial accountability for the area's railways and increase budgetary control, the old Southampton district was split into areas. District manager Harold Ward became Bournemouth's first area manager in the summer of 1966. His brief was twofold; manage the implementation of the £15 million Bournemouth electrification scheme, and either make the various legacies left by Beeching profitable or dispose of them.

Remaining railway 'stubs' now under the accountants' spotlight at Waterloo were the freight-only lines to Blandford Forum, West Moors and Ringwood. There was also the Swanage branch line which had lost its freight service the previous autumn but had not been specifically mentioned in the Beeching Report three years before.

Steam traction to Swanage ended on the fine evening of Sunday 4 September 1966, when its sub-shed of Bournemouth closed. One three-coach 'Hampshire' DEMU oper-

ated the single train service from the following day.

From early June 1967, the line below Corfe Castle was worked as a long siding with the signalbox, signals, sidings and loops taken out at Swanage. Just one track into the station remained. Staff at both Swanage and Corfe was slashed overnight. The Purbecks now had a 'basic' railway but that was not to be enough to save it.

The two minutes it took for an electric train to travel the one-and-a-half miles from Christchurch to Pokesdown stations one July morning in 1967 were to be the longest and most painful two minutes in Harold Ward's life.

Monday 10 July dawned bright. It was D-Day for the £15 million electrification scheme that promised to take the London to

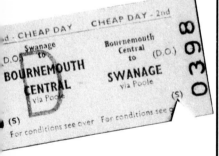

Right:
The antics surrounding the attempted hold-up of the final BR train down to Corfe Castle and Swanage by the cowboys from the Lazy C. Ranch at Creech Bottom on New Year's Day 1972, even reached the nation's tabloids. The incident and received a whole page in the Monday 3 January 1972, edition of *The Sun* **newspaper: the day that the Swanage branch line officially closed after 87 years of operation.**
Extract courtesy of The Sun

THE GREAT TRAIN UNROBBERY AT CREECH BOTTOM

The Old 98 rumbles through without a hitch and British Rail beats the bandits.

BR foils the desperadoes from the Lazy C

Guns drawn, the mean looking bunch of 'ornery critturs from the Lazy C wait for the ambush that never happened

By SUN REPORTER

THE Great Train Robbery of Creech Bottom bit the dust . . . in a big way.

Some critter tipped off the lawmen.

And when the Old 98 rumbled up to the ambush spot, they'd got the six-gun desperadoes from the Lazy C all hogtied and corralled.

The bandits were Western fans from the Lazy C riding ranch at Creech Bottom, near Wareham, Dorset. And on Saturday night they wanted to hold up British Rail's last train on the Wareham-Swanage trail.

Then, dressed as cowboys, and armed with replica six-guns, they planned to "rob" the 400 rail enthusiasts on board for charity.

Permission

Lazy C owner Alan Hunt masterminded the scheme, and claimed BR at Waterloo gave permission.

But when he checked with local station staff, the plan went drastically wrong.

They called in the local sheriff—Chief Superintendent Bill Mayo.

And when Old 98 got to Creech Bottom, he'd rounded up a posse of squad cars and officers to keep the Lazy C boys off the track.

Stretch

Alan said: "We were told that if we stopped the train, we could get a life stretch in the old hoosegow."

Wareham station manager Bill Langford said yesterday: "How on earth do you think British Rail could play silly games with these crazy idiots who spend most of their time dressed up as cowboys, playing robbers?

Sacked

"Somebody could easily have got hurt. I would have been sacked if I had condoned it."

Last night, a British Rail spokesman at Waterloo said: "We did not give permission for the train to be stopped.

"By the time we were approached it was far too late to make any arrangements.

"It's true that the last runs of trains on branch lines are usually occasions for fun and games.

"The cowboys were told that if they went on the line they would be trespassing.

"But as it happened, the whole thing went off quietly."

And nobody ended up in the hoosegow . . .

The face of '72

Her name is Jo, and she is sweet sixteen. You'll be seeing a lot of her this year

MEET HER IN THE SUN TOMORROW

'LIVER BIRDS' TEAM SPLITS

THE women comedy writers who created the BBC's Liver Birds series have split up

But Carla Lane and Myra Taylor, who also wrote ITV's Sid James comedy, Bless This House, denied yesterday that there had been a row.

Myra, of Sefton Park, Liverpool, said: "I'm working on a new idea for a television series.

'Blue movies' row at Sunday School

From JOHN SAMPSON in New York

A SUNDAY SCHOOL has been threatened with prosecution — for obscenity.

For the Unitarian school at Brookfield, Wisconsin, plans to show films of naked couples making love, and boys and girls masturbating.

The films are part of a 36-week course on sex for boys and girls aged between 12 and 14.

More than 500 mothers and fathers have signed a petition calling on the local council to stop the course.

And District Attorney Rich McConnell has warned the minister, the Rev Robert Moore, that he faces prosecution under the state's obscenity laws.

Explicit

Mr Moore says he will not back down. He told Mr McConnell the films should be as explicit as possible to let children develop their own attitudes about sex."

Bournemouth line right through to the 1980s — a day when electric replaced steam at the turn of a key.

Labour Government Transport Minister, Barbara Castle, was on board a new 12-coach electric train that was speeding at up to 100mph through Hampshire and Dorset that summer morning to start the new service.

With her was Sir Stanley Raymond, chairman of the British Railways Board, together with Mr David McKenna, General Manager of the Southern Region.

'I received a phone call from the town's fire officer,' remembers Harold Ward. 'He told me the timber decking of the river bridge at Christchurch was on fire — and it was quite serious. I couldn't believe it, on this of all days! I told the chief that I'd check it out and get straight back to him.

'I rang the signalman at Christchurch and asked where the train was. He said it was at Hinton Admiral. I decided to take a chance and delayed calling back the fire officer and hoped the bridge was not so much on fire that the train would topple into the river — taking Mrs Castle, Sir Stanley and Mr McKenna with it. It didn't and they didn't,' recalls Mr Ward with a grin.

However, the masterplan of clean and quick electric traction between London and Bournemouth and diesel push-pull trains down to Weymouth proved another nail in the Swanage branch's coffin. The 10-mile branch did not fit into the streamlined, main line picture. Electrification was out of the question according to BR. Laying third rail, altering Worgret Junction and building a 740V dc power sub-station at Corfe Castle station to 'boost the juice' down a further five miles to Swanage was too expensive to contemplate, according to management.

'Part of the deal for the investment in the electrification of the main line was the closure of the Swanage branch line and other uneconomic lines such as the "Old Road" to Ringwood and Brockenhurst and the cross-country route to Salisbury.

'I've never found much difference between Labour or Conservative governments, where the railways are concerned. Labour hasn't done much for BR — no government has. Their decisions on transport and the railways are governed by money and the electorate.

'Dorset County Council went along with the closure — or at least didn't say they were against it and sat on the fence to some extent, because they were caught between the vociferous local authorities and government policy from Whitehall.'

Harold Ward strongly rejects claims from some Purbeck councillors made at the time — principally Arthur Gaskell of Swanage UDC — that running costs, given as the reason for the closure of the Swanage line, were grossly inflated.

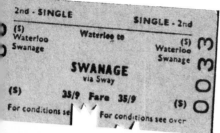

'No, that's certainly not true — they never had the facts. Local councillors tended to look at things very parochially. One had to put the fact to them that it wasn't just their parish that was affected but main line costs and the costs of central services used by the branch. It was other costs that had to be considered, not just costs incurred on the branch itself.

'One could understand the strong feelings of local people but I had to detach myself from local sympathies and approach the job as a manager. I had to take the emotion out of the thing.'

Harold Ward also vehemently rejects claims, made at the time, that British Rail changed the branch timetable and the times of main line connections to put off the travelling public from using the branch service. 'That's absolute nonsense. The timetable isn't altered to inconvenience the travelling public. It's altered to the convenience of railway operation, so the best service can be offered with the resources available. I'm sure there was no way the branch could have been saved under the present method of accountability. I don't have any regrets — it just didn't pay its way and that was that.'

Harold Ward does have one admission to make, despite his 45 years of railway experience in the south of England. 'I never thought the Swanage Railway would ever come back in the early days. I'm surprised that they have done as well as they have, but I still think their long-term aims will be a long time in coming. I don't think the Swanage Railway will ever fulfil a public train service but I do admire what they've been able to achieve over the years.'

Moreover, he does not think the Swanage Railway's park and ride ideas for taking traffic

off Purbeck's roads and putting it on to trains — similiar to a successful scheme in St Ives between BR and the Cornwall County Council — will ever work. 'There just aren't the number of people to make it viable. The Swanage Railway won't be any more than a tourist attraction — it cannot be. That's why it closed in 1972, because it just wasn't used by the travelling public.'

The painful scars of closure and redundancy dulled and soothed by the passing of time, a special piece of history was made at Swanage on New Year's Day 1992 — exactly 20 years to the day since the final BR train left the station. Swanage's final senior porter, 83-year-old Bill 'Taffy' Hazell, met Johnny Walker — the driver of that last train — for the first time since the sad evening that marked the end of an 87-year era.

Bill had the dubious privilege of blowing the last whistle and waving the last green flag to signal the final BR train away. 'Johnny hasn't changed at all — he's still the same as he was in 1972!' says a delighted Bill Hazell on Swanage station's rebuilt platform.

'I never thought that trains would come back to Swanage — never,' he adds as the pair immediately catch up on 20 years — and remember endless tales and anecdotes; all that remains of two working lifetimes on the south's railways.

Bill Hazell started his railway career at the Southern Railway's massive Eastleigh carriage and locomotive works in 1942 after being invalided out of the Army. There then followed a period as a relief porter with the end of the war. Bill began working at Swanage as a porter in 1952 when he was paid the princely sum of £4.50 for a heavy 57-hour week.

The final train, the 22.15 from Swanage, was signalled through Corfe Castle station at 22.24 by Bob Richards who became a signalman at Wareham station two days later on Monday 3 January — the day that the branch line was officially closed. Twenty years later, Bob still works in the old Southern Railway signalbox at BR Network SouthEast's restored Wareham station.

Bob Richards joined Bill Hazell and Johnny Walker for the nostalgic trip back to a reopened Swanage station, as did another of Bill's ex-colleagues, Bryan Green. He had been a booking clerk at Swanage from the mid-1950s until November 1967.

One of the passengers on that last rain had the chance to meet his driver 20 years after the sad event. William Brook from Organford, near Wareham, was one of 500 people who paid 50 pence to ride on the final six-coach DEMU train. By 1992 he was one of the keen volunteers rebuilding the Swanage branch line — and righting what many people see as the gross wrong of 1972.

Below:
A historic and moving moment. New Year's Day 1992 saw Bill 'Taffy' Hazell — Swanage station's final senior porter — meet veteran train driver Johnny Walker for the first time in 20 years. On New Day's Day, 1972, Bill waved Johnny away with the final BR train from Swanage. 'Johnny hasn't changed a bit,' says Bill with a laugh enriched by memories going back 40 years to 1952 when he started as a porter at Swanage. Left to right: 1972 'final train' passenger William Brook, now a Swanage Railway volunteer; 1950s and 1960s ex-Swanage station booking clerk Bryan Green; Corfe Castle's last signalman Bob Richards, Bill Hazell and Johnny Walker.

The Campaigner's Tale

10

'If information regarding trains is difficult to get, it's clear those trains won't be used and can be withdrawn. I'm not of a suspicious nature but I feel something may be going on.'

Don Gossling, 3 June 1964

Had a top Harley Street specialist not condemned a frail 10-year-old London girl to death, because of a serious respiratory illness, her anxious family would not have moved from the bleak environment of blitzed East London down to the seaside at Swanage in May 1945.

And, had Don and Dorothy Gossling not come to Purbeck in a desperate effort to give their daughter the chance to survive the winter, and prove her specialist wrong, the Swanage Railway would have been deprived of Don Gossling — one its most vociferous and ardent supporters some 20 years later.

But, determined little Elinor Gossling proved the specialist very wrong and did survive the winter in her new Swanage home — just yards from the branch railway line. Fifty years later she is a grandmother herself.

One summer day in 1991, a gracious, white-haired lady in a smart grey coat stands under the platform canopy at Swanage station and watches a packed steam train as it trundles and simmers its way in from Harman's Cross. The octogenarian's lively mind goes back 46 years to when, as a mother, she had her first sight of Swanage through the carriage window one Saturday afternoon. It was the end of a 136-mile journey from London with her bank manager husband, three children and the luggage that went with them. Seeing the dismal station that had gone through nearly six years of war, Dorothy wondered what she had let herself in for.

Don and Dorothy Gossling spent over 30 happy years together in Swanage, before he tragically died of a heart attack in 1977. It was Don who first suspected that the branch line was being run down prior to closure — and Don who was one of the first active members of the Isle of Purbeck Preservation Group in 1969 and then of the Swanage Railway Society in 1972. Despite the loss and the memories, Dorothy still lives in Swanage.

She has watched the railway he espoused long before it was rebuilt — or even closed — grow and prosper in front of her eyes from nothing in 1976 to the triumph of reaching Corfe Castle in 1990. 'I can remember I made woollen dollies with Elinor and read Beatrix Potter stories to her as the branch train trundled its way down to Corfe Castle and Swanage,' Dorothy recalls.

'My husband was a great believer in railways and their role in the community. We could hear and see the trains leaving Swanage station as they passed our house alongside the line in King's Road. Don hated cars because he thought they encouraged selfishness. Although we could have afforded one, we didn't buy a car and instead travelled everywhere by train.'

It was a keen-eyed Don who was the first person to notice evidence that, he claimed, proved British Railways were secretly running down the branch line in 1964. He quickly wrote to Swanage's Urban District Council, pointing out that certain train services still available were not advertised at the terminal station — including one of the Waterloo trains. He ended his letter of 3 June 1964, with an amazingly intuitive but sadly prophetic statement: 'If information regard-

Below:
Forty-six years after she got off the branch train at Swanage with her young family bound for a new home and a new life, Mrs Dorothy Gossling stands on the platform of the restored Victorian station on Saturday 1 June 1991. Champions of public transport, especially railways, Dorothy and her late husband Don were vociferous in their efforts to save the branch in the late 1960s, and then start the Swanage Railway after BR closed the line and lifted the track.
Andrew P. M. Wright

ing trains is difficult to get, it's clear those trains will not be used and can be withdrawn. I am not of a suspicious nature, but I feel something may be going on.'

In May 1965, there was another angry exchange of letters between Mr Gossling and William Bale, the long-time clerk to the Urban District Council at Swanage. Mr Gossling alleged again that current train services were not being advertised on the timetable board at Swanage, and that passengers were being discouraged from using the branch trains.

He ended his letter with a hope that was to be forlorn: 'It seems to me that these things all point to a definite attempt to run down the branch line services which, according to Dr Beeching's economics, are not profitable. I would like to suggest to the council that it's no good to wait until these policies have had effect, and then try to save the railway. What's needed is a joint policy to try and get British Railways to act as though it wanted to expand these services.'

In May 1967, anxious traders in Swanage had noticed that in British Rail's pre-electrification hype for the new London to Bournemouth main line, the Swanage branch was not shown as benefiting from the new, high-speed 'push-pull' diesel connections from Weymouth. The map showing the future rail network in Dorset did not even show the branch line at all.

Pressure mounted against the expected closure proposal by BR. Dorset County Council, Wareham Borough Council, Purbeck Rural District Council and worried hoteliers in Swanage all claimed that any road transport provided as an alternative to trains in the summer would find itself stationary, because the main A351 road was branded 'the worst road in Dorset'.

Three weeks before British Rail published its intention to close the Swanage branch line from Monday 9 September 1968, 400 local people crowded the Mowlem Theatre in Swanage on Wednesday 6 December 1967, to protest about the anticipated closure announcement.

As Swanage prepared for Christmas 1967, the town's urban district council's chairman, George Bishop, was so indignant about the closure that he threatened to parade outside the House of Commons with sandwich boards condemning BR's actions. Residents received some optimistic news and an early Christmas present on 2 December 1967. The Southern Region revealed the proposed closure of the branch was to be delayed, while the matter was considered by the rail passengers' watch-

WITHDRAWAL OF RAILWAY PASSENGER SERVICE BETWEEN WAREHAM AND SWANAGE

The Southern Region of British Railways hereby give notice that on and from Monday 3 January 1972 the railway passenger service between Wareham and Swanage will be withdrawn and Corfe Castle and Swanage stations closed.

Details of the alternative bus services are available at local railway stations and bus offices.

 British Rail | Southern

Facing page, top:
Rebuilt 'West Country' Bulleid Pacific No 34046 *Braunton* simmers at the head of the 10-coach 11.40 Swanage to London Waterloo train on Saturday 13 June 1964. Fouling the point treddle bars, the long London trains had to be started with flags from the signalbox. This shot shows the goods shed siding, the old air-raid shelter and the tracks leading to the extensive four-siding yard. Built by the Southern Railway in 1946, No 34046 *Braunton* was rebuilt in 1958 and withdrawn from BR service in 1965. *John Scrace*

Facing page, bottom:
The death throes of the Swanage branch were unmercifully long — the station being a sad, pitiful sight in its final years. Here, three-coach 'Hampshire' DEMU No 1111 leaves a 'rationalised' Swanage station on Saturday 13 June 1970, with a train for Corfe Castle and Wareham. Left with just a single line — and with the signalbox, bay track and sidings gone — Swanage was a gruesome, dismembered relic of former years.
George M. Moon.

Above left:
Twenty-one years later, the bitter, depressing memories of the branch's final, lingering years had faded thanks to the optimism and sheer hard work of the Swanage Railway volunteers. With 1931 Hunslet 0-6-0T *Cunarder* banking at the rear of the train, LSWR 'T9' class 4-4-0 No 120 of 1899 accelerates past restored carriage stock and out of Swanage station with the five-coach 12.10 train to Harman's Cross on Monday 6 May 1991.
Andrew P. M. Wright

Left:
The end of the line. After a bitter five-year fight against closure, campaigners, railway enthusiasts and the travelling public were dismayed to read on posters at Wareham, Corfe and Swanage stations in December 1971, that passenger trains were to cease the following month.
Anthony E. Trood

dog — the Transport Users Consultative Committee (TUCC) — before reporting back to the transport minister.

By the end of January 1968, over a thousand letters and petitions protesting against the closure plans had flooded into the TUCC's London offices. However, councillor George Bishop and Swanage council's clerk, Mr W. A. F. Bale, warned that the revelation was 'a cunning attempt to lull the people of Swanage and the Isle of Purbeck into a false sense of security'.

By January 1968, embarrassed council officials at Swanage were denying that 'hush, hush' talks with BR had led to a compromise solution over the future of the branch line — describing the rumours as 'utter nonsense'. It had been rumoured that the station site was to be sold and a small bus shelter-type halt set up opposite the old engine shed at Swanage.

The Public Inquiry into the closure of the branch was held at the Mowlem Theatre — within sight of the run-down station — on Tuesday 14 May 1968. Ironically, the

Mowlem Theatre would later be the scene of countless fund-raising shows over the coming years by anti-closure campaigners from the Isle of Purbeck Preservation Group. Anxiously, the TUCC emphasised it was only empowered to analyse whether and to what extent hardship to local people would be caused by the railway closure. The Inquiry could not deal with issues such as BR's reasons for closing the Swanage branch line. After the packed all-day hearing, a member of the TUCC panel anonymously told the press they thought the line was 'pretty safe', because of the volume of protests against closure.

By 10 August the verdict of the TUCC had been leaked — they unanimously supported the Isle of Purbeck against the closure, saying any replacement bus service would be 'seriously dislocated' by summer traffic jams. It now lay with the Minster of Transport to decide what to do next.

Above:
Diesel power first appeared on London to Swanage trains in the Southern Region's 1963 summer timetable. Here, Type 3 diesel-electric No 6505 (later Class 33 No 33005) coasts past King George's Playing Field and the 'up' advanced starter signal with the eight-coach 09.15 London to Swanage train on Saturday 27 August 1966. No D6505 then returned light engine to Bournemouth MPD with the steam locomotive that had been working at Swanage during the morning. 'Push-pull' fitted Class 33s regularly visited the Swanage branch until 1972. *Colin L. Caddy*

Above left:
The seeds of the Swanage Railway's future success were sown in August 1979, when volunteers started running trains over a few hundred yards of hand-laid track. Instead of a 1,550hp Class 33 diesel and eight coaches as in BR days, volunteers started with a 150hp 1957-built Fowler 0-4-0 diesel — sporting a McLaren engine — and a half-painted Southern Railway Bulleid coach built in 1947. *Mick Stone*

Campaigners' worst fears came true on 29 January when Richard Marsh revealed he was ignoring the advice of the TUCC and supporting BR's application to close the Swanage branch. The last trains would run on Saturday 4 October 1969, with closure from the following Monday. The area's three councils all angrily claimed the Minister of Transport had acted unconstitutionally in blatantly ignoring the advice of his own consumer watchdog — the TUCC.

Clearly angry at the turn of events, the clerk to Wareham and Purbeck Rural District Council said on hearing the Minister's decision: 'The councils think they have evidence that figures provided by British Rail are not accurate. It's obvious that the councils have been badly let down — and to me it's obvious that we've been sold down the river, but it's nothing more than we expected.'

Local councils decided to oppose the granting of bus licences needed to replace the branch trains in an effort to delay the closure of the Swanage line after 6 October 1969.

There was a mixture of disbelief, laughter and shock after the Southern National bus company revealed that British Rail had agreed to ration the number of tickets issued at Waterloo to just 156 for travel between Wareham and Swanage — so as not to overburden the bus service. Councillors were appalled.

South Dorset MP, Evelyn King, revealed in mid-April 1969, that he was so worried and suspicious about the alleged £68,000 loss sustained by the Swanage branch as quoted by BR, that he had asked the Ombudsman to investigate the matter urgently.

With closure now firmly set for Monday 6 October 1969, the newly-formed Isle of Purbeck Preservation Group revealed that they wanted to buy the line from BR. It was during what was assumed to be the final summer of the Swanage branch that the first seeds of the later Swanage Railway Project were sown in a small bungalow in Bay Crescent, North Swanage. 'That was when Don and I first got involved,' remembers Mrs Gossling nearly 25 years later. 'Dr Ernest Rutland wrote a letter to the local press announcing the formation of the Group and appealing for help from like-minded people. Dr Rutland and his wife, Jill, were passionate supporters of public transport and the branch line to Swanage. They had been horrified at what they saw as the deliberate running down and closure of the line. As well as Don and myself there were other local people — Moyra and Roger Cross, Eddie and Joan Noades, Bert Hickinbotham and Peter Ashton among others.'

For the next three years there were to follow countless meetings at both the Rutland's

house and 'Belvedere', the home of Don and Dorothy Gossling, which were to become the Bethlehem of the later Swanage Railway. It was revealed that the Group were 'impressed' by promises of financial support from the people of Swanage. But, they were cruelly rebuffed by Wareham's Borough Council, which described their plans as not being a 'viable proposition' and refused any grant aid.

The Group wanted to buy the entire branch line and negotiate with the Southern Region of BR for 'running rights' along the main line into Wareham. There would be an all-year-round diesel service using redundant ex-BR DMUs as well as steam haulage to Corfe Castle during the summer. There would also be an exhibition centre and museum at Swanage station. Ten people would be employed, including conductor-guards who would collect fares, as well as other qualified staff for driving, signalling and track maintenance. Voluntary labour would be recruited to maintain buildings, fences, earthworks and drainage, they said.

By the autumn of 1969, the refusal of the local authorities to grant bus licences to replace the trains between Swanage and Wareham delayed the branch closure to 5 January 1970, and then to Saturday 2 May. An angry Dorset County Council spokesman claimed British Rail's statements on the resultant traffic chaos after the line was closed were misleading and could have unduly affected the Minister's decision. The council spokesman added that traffic on the main but winding A351 Wareham to Swanage road was expected to increase by a massive 70% by 1975.

Swanage and Corfe Castle residents reeled with shock when they read in their local newspapers on 15 September 1969, that the Ombudsman backed the Minister and British Rail. With the Southern Region now declaring that the branch would close on 2 May 1970, Swanage Urban District Council made an impassioned plea for the line to be retained through the summer of 1970.

In mid-January 1970, the Southern Region revealed it would not be closing the Swanage branch line until the following September, because traffic commissioners in London had not yet given permission for the replacement bus services, due to continued objections by the area's local authorities. But, the repeated stays of execution for the branch line were proving a problem for the Isle of Purbeck Group. A spokesman revealed in December 1970, that the repeated shifts by the Southern Region — causing unfounded optimism for the safety of the branch and reducing enthusiasm for a private buy-out — had caused a well-known national company to withdraw its planned support for the Group's fight. The

Above:
A peaceful branch line scene that many will remember from their childhood in the 1940s, 1950s and early 1960s. With lineside embankments almost manicured, Victorian 'M7' 0-4-4T No 30106 of 1905 steams up the 1 in 132 gradient towards the A351 Afflington road bridge between Harman's Cross and Corfe Castle with an afternoon train from Swanage to Wareham on Saturday 8 August 1953. In tow is a two-coach LSWR 'push-pull' set that offered the novelty of Edwardian travel as late as the 1950s. *R.R. Bowler/ Courtesy Mike Smith collection*

Left:
Swanage Railway volunteers determinedly relay the track between Woodyhyde Farm and the A351 Afflington road bridge en route from Harman's Cross station to Corfe Castle. During their marathon 10-day effort, they managed to lay over half a mile of track from Woodyhyde to Corfe Common. Here, an ex-Southern Railway 15-ton diesel-electric carefully positions a 60ft track panel on the newly cleared trackbed. *Andrew P. M. Wright*

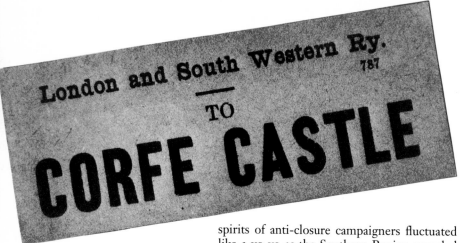

spirits of anti-closure campaigners fluctuated like a yo-yo as the Southern Region revealed in January 1971 that the end of the Swanage line was to be deferred, yet again, and this time until the autumn.

Finally, on Saturday 6 November 1971, the Southern Region announced the last trains would run down to Corfe Castle and Swanage on New Year's Day, Saturday 1 January 1972 — closure taking effect from the following Monday morning. Swanage councillors begged British Rail to keep the Swanage line during the summer of 1972 as a feeder to the £590,000 grant-aided Bournemouth to Weymouth line. Councillors claimed that if closed, the main line would be robbed of more than £40,000 a year in contributory income earned at Corfe Castle and Swanage.

Through the dying days of 1971, British Rail issued a stern ultimatum. They would be willing to keep the line open, but only if local authorities backed up their indignant protests with money and paid over £100,000 to the Southern Region. If this was not done, BR said the closure date would stay.

Local councillors were furious and demanded to see a detailed breakdown of the line's alleged losses and running expenses from British Rail.

In late December 1971, Dorset County Council said 'no' to British Rail's 'ransom' of £100,000 to stop the Swanage line closing. They also rebuffed the Isle of Purbeck Preservation Group, one councillor from Studland branding their efforts as 'a first class con' and saying 'it would be disaster if BR gave running rights to these people'. Councillors agreed that if British Rail closed the line, the county council would purchase the trackbed between Furzebrook and Northbrook Road bridge at Swanage station for a Corfe by-pass as well as for road improvements at the Victoria Avenue road bridge.

With talks between British Rail and local authorities grinding to a halt, the Isle of Purbeck Preservation Group announced it was being forced to give up its three-year fight in April 1972. Their project was abandoned amongst bitterness and frustration with

British Rail and the County Council. But, just a few months later, that fury and anger was to be channelled into another group that would, eventually, succeed.

The Group's volunteers had been unable to raise the £115,000 required by BR as well as a non-returnable deposit of £11,500 for the loss of interest on the scrap value of the seven miles of track.

British Rail's breakdown of their £115,000 came to £45,000 for the land between Worgret Junction and Northbrook Road bridge, but not including the station. On top of that, £70,000 was asked for the redundant bullhead track, which Group members claimed was an over-inflated price. Around £40,000 would be needed for new stations at Worgret Junction and Swanage if the Victorian terminal station was sold by BR for future redevelopment.

The Group was caught in a frustrating catch 22 situation. British Rail were only willing to negotiate if the Group had the backing of Dorset County Council — and the County Council said they would only negotiate if the Group was given 'running rights' by BR to run trains into Wareham and ran an all-year amenity train service on the branch at the earliest opportunity.

While winding up the Group's affairs in the summer of 1972 — as the tracks at Swanage and Corfe were being torn up — chairman Mr Tonkin wrote to a long-time member, Gerry Andrews, of Wareham. 'We're more than sorry at having to abandon the project but I feel the committee were right as there is nothing more we can do. Without ready cash of over £100,000 we don't have a chance — and now, no doubt, with the government grant the Corfe Castle by-pass will go through. I feel quite sick at the turn of events but am glad that we tried.'

Against all the odds and proving the Jonahs and cynics wrong, a by-pass did not obliterate the railway at Corfe and 20 years later; the road has still not been built. The Swanage Railway has relaid its tracks to the Victorian station and the County Council chosen a 'far east' route for the by-pass that avoids using the railway land.

'I do wish Don, Dr Rutland and his wife Jill — all dead now — could see the railway in the 1990s,' muses Dorothy. 'I know they'd be so thrilled to see full-length trains running up to Harman's Cross packed with passengers. It's a great shame they aren't here to see the fruits of all their hard work.

'I did what I did to help raise money for the Swanage Railway, because my husband was in love with the railway — and I was in love with him. It was as simple as that,' she says with a wistful sparkle in her eyes.

The Railwaymen's Tale

'The closure decision has been made by railway officials trying to justify their own existence and cover their disastrous years of mismanagement.'

Fred Norman

'The loss is very much less than they claim. They could have made the line pay, if they'd set out to sell rail travel instead of letting things slide.'

Jack Cannons

The shock decision by the Labour Government to axe the Swanage line in January 1969, was not only greeted with abject horror by the people of Purbeck — it also prompted two branch railwaymen to break the silence amongst colleagues and speak their minds on the controversial issue.

Fred Norman had been working trains between Wareham and Swanage since the late 1940s and was, in 1969, a driver based at Bournemouth, who drove the 'Hampshire' DEMU trains on the branch in its final years. He angrily branded the government decision by Transport Minister, Richard Marsh, as being 'blatantly wrong' and claimed it made Purbeck 'a sacrificial goat'.

'The closure decision had been made by railway officials trying to justify their own existence and cover their disastrous years of mismanagement — and by Ministry of Transport officials that can never have been near the area to see for themselves the terrible road conditions, which they intend to greatly increase,' Fred angrily wrote in a letter to the *Bournemouth Evening Echo*.

'Into all this the Minister intends to add the extra buses and other traffic for the holiday railway travellers. The Minister stated that if the railway traveller pays for a reserved seat then this will count on the buses as well. Very nice on paper, but what about the outgoing travellers? Knowing the railways as I do, I feel it is extremely unlikely that the trains at Wareham will wait for more than a minute for a bus.

'It is no good the Minister saying that some delay will occur on a few Saturdays in the season. Late in September 1968, I left Swanage at 18.05 to catch the 19.23 from Wareham and because of the traffic, never made it. And that was in mid-week!' he added.

'To me, the most disturbing point is what man has the right to deny anyone — who is unfortunate to have a serious accident in this area during the summer months — the right to get the best possible treatment because the delay on the road is such that the journey is, if not impossible, extremely long to Poole Hospital.

'The Transport Minister said he would take account of this proposed closure when considering any road plans in the future. This, surely, is putting the cart before the horse. We must have improved roads before the closure adds any increase to the traffic,' he continued.

'Richard Marsh has, no doubt, based his decision on the figures submitted by the Railways Board; and what an inflated set of figures they turn out to be. I understand one item was £30,000 for signalling. If this relates to the past it was only wasted as the system had only just been renewed at Swanage when it was torn up for scrap. If it relates to the future, it's even more of a farce as the branch needs only one colour-light signal at Worgret Junction. There need never be more than one train on the line at any one time.

'It's upon inflated figures such as this that the Minister bases his opinion that it is not justifiable to give such a large subsidy to keep open such a small length of line, and rightly so, any subsidy would be like feeding a donkey on strawberries. If the subsidy was £20,000 this year it would have to be £40,000 next year and so on. This is not the answer.

'I am all in favour of closing any line that cannot pay its way, but only after every possible economy has been made in an effort to achieve this. Only half-hearted attempts have been made at economy on the Swanage line. What other 10 miles of single line in the British Isles requires four signalmen per day to run it?

'The answer is to give a block grant, firstly, to put half barriers at Wareham level crossing — the same as are in operation at Brocken-

Above:

With choking weeds invading the once tidy ballast by the 'up' starter signal at Corfe Castle, three-coach 'Hampshire' DEMU No 1128 noisily whines out of the cutting through the Purbeck Hills and trundles into the station with the 16.44 Wareham to Swanage train on a sunny Thursday 7 August 1969. *John Scrace*

Top right:

The railway returns to Corfe Castle station. On the fine evening of Thursday 27 September 1990, the Swanage Railway's track-relaying train sits by the stripped 'up' starter signal. Behind the train, the East Hill of the Purbecks looms large. On board the 'Dolphin' flat wagon, a 60ft track panel waits to be laid. The 15-ton diesel-electric crane was built in 1947 for the Southern Railway and the Southampton Docks. *Andrew P. M. Wright*

Above right:

Swanage station in the declining years of steam traction and a scene that many hoped would be recreated after the line was closed and lifted. On the warm early evening of Tuesday 9 June 1964, a grimy ex-LMS Ivatt 2-6-2T No 41238 waits to leave Swanage's platform 1 with the three-coach 17.38 to Corfe Castle and Wareham. Beyond the stopblocks to the left can be seen the 'Railway Hotel'. To the right is the bay platform and goods shed siding with, beyond, the large goods yard and carriage sidings. *John Scrace*

hurst. This would speed up the flow of traffic. Secondly, instal power points at Worgret Junction, worked from Wareham. Keep two porters and a booking clerk at Swanage and run the whole line from Wareham signalbox.

'The power points, besides cutting out the two signalboxes at Worgret and Corfe Castle, would enable the running time to be cut from 20 to 18 minutes thus making it possible to make more connections at Wareham with Weymouth and London trains. That would make the line more attractive to the public.

'A second-hand one-sided concrete platform could be put behind Court Road with a small waiting room and booking office with the line stopping under the Northbrook Road bridge. This would enable the whole of the station site to be cleared and run, if necessary, by the council on a 50/50 profit-sharing basis. This would help the economic side of the line as well as the town.

'Swanage, Corfe Castle and Wareham — and even Dorchester and Weymouth, for they are next — must form an action committee to fight these closures. They should invite the Minister to come and see for himself, this summer, the chaos he so lightly dismisses. Everyone must implore him to think again.

'We do not fear, as some must, a close examination of the cost figures given by the Railway Board. They must be made to explain them in detail; then perhaps they will change them once again.

'I challenge any officials, transport, railway or any other, to openly contest any of the facts or proposals in this letter, for people in this area must demand only one thing — Justice,' Fred ended impassionately.

British Rail and its alleged shoddy treatment of the Swanage line came in for further stinging criticism after the branch timetable was

changed yet again — and through trains to Bournemouth, Southampton and London withdrawn completely in early October 1969.

A railwayman for 40 years, 57-year-old Jack Cannons had been the station foreman at Swanage station from 1963 until 6 October 1969, when he was made redundant. Many claimed that he, like other loyal railwaymen, was a victim of a premeditated attempt to run down and close the branch line, no matter what. Mr Cannons alleged that British Rail had deliberately let the branch 'go to pot' and that the Southern Region could have made the line pay, if they had really wanted to. He angrily dismissed BR's claim that the Swanage branch lost £79,000 during 1968 as 'bunkum'.

'The loss is very much less than they claim,' he told the *Bournemouth Evening Echo* and *Swanage Times* newspapers in early October 1969. 'They could have made the line pay if they'd set out to sell rail travel instead of letting things slide,' he added.

'To be fair, they did offer me a transfer. One job was a porter at Dorchester, but all the jobs they offered me would have been subject to redundancy within a short time. I said I wanted to stay in this area. They said I could go on living in the station house at Corfe Castle.

'What makes me so bitter is that there was no need to let the line run down. When I came here six years ago, the trains were packed with people. Sacking me is typical of the way they are letting things go to pot. Stations are dirty — they just won't keep the staff to clean them. And now they've taken off the through trains to London.

'I quite agree the line could not be made to pay on traffic to Swanage alone, but they could run Pied Piper excursions — a 30 shilling day trip with free travel for an accompanying child under 14 years of age — like the Western Region do. Corfe Castle and Swanage would be popular destinations. They used to run excursions down here and they always did very well.

'Another thing they could do is to run very cheap trains to London for shopping and so on. They could cut the fares a lot. At present, they do a cheap day trip to London for two pounds and six shillings instead of the usual three pounds and ten shillings. But, they make too many restrictions like saying you can only travel when there are slow trains to Waterloo. If they made it possible to catch the fast midday train there would be more customers. They'd have to bring back the customers anyway, so why not make 46 shillings the standard fare?'

Jack repeatedly claimed the alleged deficit sustained by the Swanage branch train service was exaggerated, because passengers to Swanage often booked on long-distance trains — not only to London and the Midlands but to Scotland as well.

'But all Swanage is credited for is 12 shillings return. The high-ups don't seem to realise that if people can't go all the way by train, they'd sooner use their car instead. They won't go to Wareham, pay for parking and then go the rest of the way by train.'

The ex-station foreman at Swanage, Jack had started his railway career at the age of 15 — cleaning station lamps. He claimed there was too much of what he called 'top brass' management in British Rail who, he alleged, were earning high salaries at a time when the industry was being cut back.

'In the old days, the station master was the boss, and we knew it. These days, we have not only the station manager, but also the area and district managers coming down to see us — and being paid for it.'

'Before the war, the job of a railwayman was a coveted job that demanded and got respect. Now it's just a music hall joke,' added Jack as he looked forlornly at Swanage's empty station platform — the paint peeling off the canopy and the loop, bay track and sidings all long lifted.

'But,' he added on that autumn day in 1969, 'I will miss my work here, because it brought me in contact with people. It's surprising how many of them need help and get into trouble. Now, I'll have to look for another job, where I can still meet people.'

Jack Cannons' outburst came at the end of a week that Swanage Urban District Council's Arthur Gaskell condemned British Rail for their treatment of local people and the council. He maintained that the alleged losses BR

incurred in running the Swanage branch were falsely inflated to justify closure. He told fellow councillors that BR had informed the Government Ombudsman, called in to investigate the closure, that the deficit had increased from £65,000 in 1967 to £79,000 in 1968 — largely, they claimed, because of new pay awards.

'That's ridiculous and totally absurd,' he spat angrily. 'There are 12 men employed on the branch and the 21% increase in running costs was more than the total salaries of all 12 men.'

They included two porters and a clerk at Swanage, the station foreman just made redundant, two signalmen at Corfe Castle station, two drivers and two guards. The 10-mile line also had the use of two track maintenance men.

Councillor Gaskell also scoffed at BR's claim of £31,500 — over £3,000 a mile — as the cost of track maintenance and signalling on the branch line. Instead, he claimed the true figure was just a tenth of that — around £300 a mile. 'I have a good source for my figures and they've been most carefully checked,' said Councillor Gaskell at the time. As a comparison, he cited the A351 Swanage to Wareham road, which often carried over a thousand vehicles an hour in 1969 and cost only £850 a mile to maintain. A quarter of that figure was for widening and repairs.

However, despite the avalanche of criticism from the public, local authorities and even railway employees, British Rail was unrepentant. The opinion of a British Rail spokesman in London to the *Bournemouth Evening Echo* was curt and to the point. 'We don't enter into any discussion about figures. These are drawn up in accordance with a formula laid down by the Minister of Transport. We have done all we can to sell this service — and Swanage has cheap day tickets to any station on the Southern Region. It has not been successful.'

Below:
Corfe Castle station swelters in the heat of a July afternoon in 1987 as thick undergrowth envelops the 'up' and 'down' platforms. Looking towards the cutting through the Purbeck Hills on Saturday 4 July 1987, the Victorian platform is to the left and the 'down' platform station sign just visible above the rising undergrowth to the right. Faced with this sight, many people thought the Swanage Railway's aim of bringing the trains back was a ridiculous pipe dream. *Andrew P. M. Wright*

Below right:
The vision becomes a reality and the sceptics are forced to eat their doubting words. Ex-LSWR 'T9' class 4-4-0 No 120 gently eases her way into the 'down' platform at Corfe Castle station on Friday 10 May 1991, with an engineering train from Swanage and Harman's Cross. No 120 was on a 10-year loan from the National Railway Museum and the first ex-BR steam locomotive to run into the station since the afternoon of Sunday 18 June 1967. The main through line has been laid but the 'up' loop line still waits to be installed. *Andrew P. M. Wright*

The Councillor's Tale

12

'If democracy means anything in this country, we're entitled to know just what defence the Ministry has for its conduct in this matter. The whole thing stinks.'

Councillor Arthur Gaskell

Vociferous Swanage councillor Arthur Gaskell was a painful and annoying thorn in the side of British Rail during their five-year battle to close the Purbeck branch line, because he claimed to have embarrassing information that proved BR was deliberately and repeatedly exaggerating its losses. The vocal chairman of the Urban District Council's works committee periodically and bluntly accused the Railways Board in London of 'juggling the figures' and making 'a blunder'.

The late Mr Gaskell claimed that his information was accurate and came from a reputable 'local' source. But, he would not reveal where he obtained it — a secret he finally took with him to the grave in the mid-1970s, when the new Swanage Railway Society was battling to gain a foothold at Swanage station.

The evening that two packed 'Hampshire' DEMUs forming the final train trundled up to Wareham from Swanage and Corfe Castle on New Year's Day 1972, he angrily described the branch as having been 'killed off by a formula' devised by faceless London civil servants in 1968.

He alleged the new accountancy method for determining whether railways were 'paying their way' transformed a profitable branch line making a healthy surplus of £25,000 a year into a massive loss-maker — going into the red by a huge £173,000 in an instant and becoming ripe for closure.

Mr Gaskell maintained that the Swanage branch was the first line to be closed which had earned — between 1967 and 1972 — more than the operational expenditure incurred in providing the necessary train services. And once the Minister of Transport, Richard Marsh, had agreed to the closure of the line in 1969 — ignoring the advice of his own inspector and the Transport Users Consultative Committee — it took another three years actually to effect it.

'The British Railways Board have provided, at various times, four separate itemised financial statements,' he told the *Swanage Times*. 'In only one case do the statistics follow a consistent pattern — and none of them can be justified on the basis of accountancy methods used in the Beeching Report.'

Mr Gaskell admitted the Swanage branch was running at a loss until the end of steam traction in September 1966. But, he said the end of the goods service on 4 October 1965, the cessation of the two train service, the change to diesel units and the reduction of staff at Swanage from 12 to five and then down to just three by 1969 — together with the unstaffed status of Corfe from September 1968 — all helped to put the Swanage branch in the black.

'The first figure given for expenditure, provided in December 1967, was £48,000. That probably referred to 1965 when there was a much larger staff and the expensive and labour-intensive steam traction was used. The figure given for income was £19,800.

'The actual annual operational expenditure can be calculated — either by estimating the costs of running the diesel train service, manning Swanage station, track maintenance etc, or alternatively by using the generally accepted assumption that total labour costs of between £11,000 and £12,000 per annum represent 60% of the total operational expenditure. Both methods give a figure between £19,000 and £20,000 for annual expenditure in providing the train service through 1967.'

However, from January 1968, a completely new method of accountancy was introduced for the purposes of obtaining government subsidies. It was the result of the recommendations of the Joint Steering Group, contained in the White Paper 'Railway Policy', presented to Parliament in 1967.

'In addition to operational expenditure and interest on capital already expended in providing the existing stations, rolling stock etc, the British Railways were allowed to include a

Above:
An all-time low in the history of the Swanage Railway. A workman from scrap merchants Eagre & Co of Scunthorpe, cuts up track at the Swanage end of the Corfe Castle station loop with his oxyacetylene torch on the fine afternoon of Monday 10 July 1972 — the first day of track-lifting. Foreman David Meeham told the *Bournemouth Evening Echo* newspaper that day: 'British Rail asked us to start as quickly as we could. We'll have it lifted within five weeks'. *Arthur Grant*

A typical scene at Wareham station that would be gone with the end of steam traction on the branch in September 1966. The fireman holds the hose with the guard looking on from the platform as ex-LMS Ivatt 2-6-2T No 41312 takes water at Wareham's 'down' main platform during the summer of 1964. After taking water, No 41312 ran round her two-coach Maunsell carriage set before reversing into the south bay platform 1 and departing with a morning train for Corfe Castle and Swanage. *John Lakey*

The massive diesel engine of a BR Class 47 locomotive idles at Wareham station's down platform on Saturday 6 July 1991, before departing with an inter-regional train from Manchester to Weymouth. Getting off the train clutching his bucket and spade, a young boy was heard to tell the guard proudly: 'I'm off to Swanage with my mum and dad'. Nineteen years before, he could have gone the whole way by train. Class 47 diesels (known as Type 4s in the 1960s) worked down to Corfe Castle and Swanage in 1965 and 1966 on the summer Sunday through train from Eastleigh.
Andrew P. M. Wright

figure for depreciation. This was assessed on a replacement cost basis,' claimed Councillor Gaskell.

'The effect of this new change was illustrated by Mr Gerrard Fiennes — former General Manager of the BR's Eastern Region — in January 1969. He claimed the Steering Group's new formula turned a profit of £25,000 on the working of one branch line into a deficit of £173,000.'

Swanage Urban District Council received BR's financial breakdown of the line's alleged costs over the period 1968 and 1969 from the Department of Transport.

'The figure given for movement on the branch was £25,000 in 1968 and £32,000 in 1969. These figures were two to three times the actual costs. Terminal or station costs were said to be £19,000 in 1969, when it had a staff of just four people. This annual figure

was greater than the total capital costs of constructing the actual stations in 1884. £15,000 was the figure given as being interest and administration charges for 1969. This includes the addition of 12.5% of total expenditure for central administration costs. These are in excess of the total wage bill for those employed on the branch line!

'Finally, the costs of track and signalling in 1968 — bearing in mind Swanage was reduced to just one track and all signals at the terminal station had been taken out in 1967 — was £35,000 for 1968. This was later reduced to £34,000 in 1969, because the Ministry of Transport regarded the original figure as being too high.'

However, in December 1971, when Swanage UDC asked for details of the amount of subsidy required to keep the line open during 1972, the British Railways Board submitted a figure of £71,000 for track and signalling.

'This was sub-divided into £58,000 for track and £13,000 for signalling. As track maintenance was carried out by members of a small gang based at Wareham on the Bournemouth to Weymouth main line, the actual amount of maintenance has been estimated as being equivalent to less than two men's work. A figure of £3,000 should cover labour and materials.

'Signalling was effected by the carrying of a single-line tablet from Worgret Junction to Corfe Castle. A figure of £3,000 a year should have covered the wages of the signalmen employed — and a substantial proportion of this should have been borne by the ball clay traffic to Furzebrook, which earns the line over £50,000 a year.

'The actual receipts at Swanage station in 1968 were said to be £28,995. This did not include any income from the season tickets of 135 grammar school pupils or of 52 college students who travelled on the line twice a day.

'Also, no income was received from 80 to 90% of over 5,000 summer visitors, who booked return tickets to Corfe and Swanage at their home stations. Only the fare for the branch journey from Wareham down to Swanage was attributed to the branch. In 1968, BR maintained the income from the whole branch to be £20,000.'

Councillor Gaskell claimed the Ministry of Transport paid subsidies to British Rail on the basis of certified branch deficits of £65,000 in 1968, £79,000 in 1969. In December 1971, the local authorities were asked to contribute an annual subsidy of £109,000 to prevent closure of the line.

'Certainly, if similar accounting methods were adopted by local authorities — and depreciation on a replacement cost basis — was applied to roads and buildings then the rates levelled, council houses and road fund licences could easily be doubled.

'I have made a number of accusations about what British Rail have done. I have challenged their figures and made very serious allegations. Not one word has been said in their defence by either BR or the Ministry of Transport. I can only assume my statements were correct and the BR spokesman was not in a position to contradict them.'

Corfe Castle station in limbo — just nine days before track-lifting operations were scheduled to begin. 'Push-pull' fitted Class 33 diesel-electric locomotive No D6580 (later No 33119) idles at the station's 'down' platform with a special lineside hut-clearing train on Friday 23 June 1972. With a steam crane from Eastleigh — later preserved on the Mid-Hants Railway in Hampshire — and four flat wagons, No D6580 spent the day salvaging four concrete lineside huts between Corfe and Swanage. *Anthony E. Trood*

With the prospect that the Victorian station at Swanage was going to be demolished — just weeks after the final train had left — to make way for a large retail, commercial and leisure facility with car parking — Arthur Gaskell once again launched a vociferous and heartfelt attack in characteristic style.

'The Ministry contributed £13,000 in 1968 and £15,000 in 1969 towards the upkeep of the station — in the full knowledge all along that they were going to close it down. It's an "Alice in Wonderland" situation.

'If democracy means anything in this country we are entitled to know just what defence the Ministry has for its conduct in this matter — the whole thing stinks.'

Centre right:

A sad sight at Corfe Castle station during the first week of August 1972, and looking towards Wareham from the point into the goods yard. Contractors Eagre & Co of Scunthorpe are well advanced with track-lifting. The 'down' line was temporarily retained so that a flat wagon and open wagons could be filled with scrap before being hauled up to Furzebrook and Wareham by a BR Class 33 diesel. Starting on Monday 10 July 1972, the 6½ miles of track from Swanage to Norden were gone by the middle of August. *Gerry Andrews*

Right:

What nature can do in just 15 years if left to run riot. Corfe Castle station lies asleep under choking undergrowth one hot summer lunchtime in July 1986. A huge pine tree dwarfs the stationmaster's tiny garden. Swanage station's foreman, Jack Cannons, lived in the stationmaster's house at Corfe from 1963 until 1976, when he moved away as the undergrowth grew ever higher outside his windows. *Andrew P. M. Wright*

The Angry Young Man's Tale

13

'It was quite incredible — like something out of a James Bond film. I suddenly received a brown envelope stuffed with confidential copies of correspondence between British Rail and the scrap merchants. It was anonymously signed "003 and a half".'

Andrew Goltz

It is a still, warm May afternoon in 1972 — a year remembered for the international revulsion of the Munich Olympics massacre, the heady music of Marc Bolan's T-Rex, the bitter miners' strike against Tory Prime Minister, Ted Heath, and the excitement of the first commercially available pocket calculator and digital watch.

Two long-haired university students casually wander along the silent, weed-ridden platforms at Corfe Castle station — unaware of the history they were about to make, or the effect their decision was to have on the next six years of their lives. The tracks are silent — with a thin, matt brown, almost mauve film of rust, where just a few months before there was a gleaming silver shine. The first six months of 1972 were strange — a limbo period when the Swanage branch line awaited its fate. The packed final train had moaned and whined its way from Swanage late on the evening of New Year's Day 1972.

Would the tracks below Furzebrook be lifted and the railway lost forever below a Corfe Castle by-pass or would the railway line be saved to become another Severn Valley or Bluebell?

It was anybody's guess in the political climate of the early 1970s, when road ruled rail and environmentalism was generally in its infancy; but two young men in their early 20s thought differently.

The warm summer breeze gently blows from the village against Andrew Goltz's bearded face. The sound of traffic grinding its way along the main A351 road through the village drifts up to the railway station as he gazes into the middle distance and thinks.

'We can do something with this, you know. We've got to,' Andrew mutters as he turns to his friend, a young London psychology student. 'We can't let all this be covered by a by-pass and car park, can we?' he asks his friend who is kicking the grass as he studiously looks for buried railway remains.

Andrew Goltz was and is an incredible character in anybody's book — the man who formed the Swanage Railway Society and kick-started the Swanage Railway's Purbeck Line into action.

Had his parents decided to return to their home in Soviet-held Poland after the end of World War 2 — and doubtless been shot by the nervous Communist authorities of the new Russian satellite — or started a new life on a South American farm, then the Swanage Railway might not be in existence today.

But, luckily for supporters of the rebuilt Purbeck Line, Polish cavalry officer Gustav Goltz and his anti-Nazi resistance fighter wife, Ursula, decided to emigrate to Britain after the defeat of Hitler in the spring of 1945.

It was three holidays to Swanage in the mid-1950s that first introduced the London youngster to the delights of a typical Southern Railway branch line; and planted the seeds of a remarkable story of human determination, pin-sharp vision and the plain refusal to take 'no' for an answer that was to start the embryonic Swanage Railway some 15 years later. 'It was idyllic and it later seemed unthinkable

Below:
Nineteen years after they first met as BR tore up the Swanage branch's tracks, the dynamic founder of the Swanage Railway Society, Andrew Goltz, chats to long-time Swanage Railway campaigner Dorothy Gossling at Swanage station on Saturday 1 June 1991.
Andrew P. M. Wright

that the Swanage branch line could go. I suppose that's what spurred me on to try and save and then rebuild the Swanage line nearly 20 years later,' remembers Andrew, who is now a computer consultant with the Automobile Association at their Reading headquarters.

Having read that the Swanage branch line had finally closed after a bitter five-year battle, Andrew was spurred on to try and do something to save the line from oblivion. In doing so, he involved a Polish friend from his early 1960s school days in Ealing — John Sloboda — who was by 1972 a psychology student at Oxford University.

One sunny Saturday afternoon in May 1972, they drove down from London with the intention of walking the branch track and inspecting all the major features to ascertain whether saving the line was a worthwhile and viable project. They soon realised that it was.

Andrew Goltz and John Sloboda decided there and then to form the Swanage Railway Society with the intention of persuading British Rail not to lift the tracks and instead sell both the track and land to the Society.

The Society announced its plans to the press and public on Tuesday 13 June 1972, just two weeks before the end of the six-month limbo period, during which BR could

Facing page, top:
A view that generations of drivers and firemen took for granted but which was to disappear in 1972. This driver's-eye view of Corfe Castle station was taken from the cab of a 'Hampshire' three-coach DEMU as it clattered down the 1 in 80 gradient from Swanage, past the 'up' home signal and into the passing loop on a warm lunchtime during the summer of 1969. The long weed-ridden headshunt for the goods yard is to the left. In the foreground is where the scrap merchants started lifting the track on Monday 10 July 1972. *Chris Phillips*

Facing page, bottom:
The acrid smell of oxyacetylene cutting torches strikes the senses as the sharp ringing sound of keys being hammered out of the track chairs drifts in the warm summer air at Corfe Castle station. The sound of steel-capped boots slipping on the ballast echoes down the rusty track as the workmen of Eagre & Co crowbar the rails out of the chairs on Monday 10 July 1972. This was the first day of track-lifting on the Swanage branch. *Arthur Grant*

Above left:
Exactly 18 years to the day that the track was lifted, the rails of the Swanage Railway are relayed by volunteers into Corfe Castle station — on the same spot as the previous picture. Here on Tuesday 10 July 1990, progress on laying the Swanage end point is well advanced. In reaching the five-mile point at Corfe Castle station, volunteers had laid over 2,500 tonnes of track from Swanage — 900 rails and 11,000 sleepers with over 70,000 bolts and 22,000 track chairs. *Andrew P. M. Wright*

not touch the track, came to an end. They would restore a complete service by 1974 and £150,000 would be needed to buy the line from BR and start a train service. Half the amount would come through public subscription and around 800,000 people would be using the line every year by 1975, it was predicted.

A tourist service using steam locomotives would be run between Swanage and Furzebrook with halts at Blue Pool and Harman's Cross. Efforts would be made to purchase the three-mile Furzebrook to Worgret Junction section of line from BR during the two-year timescale. 'Running rights' along the main line into Wareham would be negotiated in return for BR using the Society's line to Furzebrook free of charge for its clay traffic.

It was also planned to buy the south bay platform at Wareham station from BR within the two-year timescale of the plan. Once up and running, the new Swanage Railway would provide steam train services for tourists and visitors during the summer, which would subsidise a diesel amenity train service for local people throughout the rest of the year.

The British Rail Property Board's swift response to the Society's new proposals was to ask for an immediate £11,500 interest payment on the value of the track — which British Rail claimed to be £115,000 — while talks over purchasing continued. Track-lifting was delayed from the intended starting date of Sunday 2 July 1972, but only for eight days. In the event, operations started at Corfe station on Monday 10 July 1972.

The Society said it would pay the interest on the scrap value of the seven miles of track, but only after an independent assessment. Such were the howls of protest when contractors suddenly started lifting at Corfe that a wave of angry telegrams and letters was unleashed by the local council, the Society and local people. Intended targets were British Rail's Chairman, Richard Marsh, and Environment Secretary, Peter Walker.

However, as contractors Eagre & Co of Scunthorpe moved in to tear up the seven miles of single line between Swanage, Corfe Castle and Furzebrook, British Rail had to cope with an embarrassing leak from their London headquarters.

A 'deep throat', who humorously signed himself '003 and a half', claimed he had evidence to show that the price of track as sold to the scrap merchants was only £50,000 and not the claimed value of £115,000 as quoted by BR to the Society.

Right:
Diesel power at Swanage in the last years of steam traction. On the warm afternoon of Saturday 14 August 1965, Type 3 diesel-electric locomotive No D6530 (later Class 33 No 33018) in early 1960s green livery idles in the station headshunt by the Victorian engine shed. The crew of No D6530 are waiting for the branch train to arrive from Corfe Castle before returning to Bournemouth MPD light engine. *Colin L. Caddy.*

Below:
This is what student Andrew Goltz faced as he tried to persuade local people and authorities that he could give Swanage back its railway. The weed-ridden trackbed by the disused engine shed at Swanage station lies silent on the fine evening of Friday 12 September 1975. Looking towards the Northbrook Road bridge — with the demolished platform and goods shed beyond — the engine shed, turntable pit and coaling dock are nearly obscured by the huge elm trees.
George M. Moon

'It was quite incredible — rather like something out of a James Bond film. We never did find out who the person was,' says Andrew Goltz. 'One day I received this ordinary looking brown manilla envelope in the post. In it were stuffed copies of all the communications and letters between the British Rail Property Board in London and the scrap merchants Eagre & Co of Scunthorpe. We couldn't believe it.'

Although the avalanche of paper protests did not stop the rails from being lifted and the sleepers gouged out of the ballast, it did achieve one thing. That was a sudden request for the Society to see the head of BR's Property Board in London for face-to-face talks.

When his secretary rang through to say Mr Goltz and Mr Sloboda of the Swanage Railway Society were waiting to see him, Robert Lawrence was, no doubt, expecting to see two middle-aged and perhaps slightly eccentric businessmen walk into his plush office.

But, his thoughts were interrupted — and the executive more than a little taken aback — when he saw two young students confidently breeze into his office. At one point the two students tried hard not to smile, when Mr Lawrence asked them to 'turn off the tap', so that the flow of objecting letters, telegrams

and phone calls that were deluging him over the tracklifting would stop.

'We were successful in persuading him to order the contractors to stop lifting operations half a mile short of their target at Furzebrook — leaving a useful half-mile spur for our future track relaying train. Mr Lawrence also agreed to leave all the ballast down on the six-and-a half mile section, the signal posts, the waiting shelter and other structures at Corfe Castle and Swanage. For that we had to pay a sum based on the notional interest of their value — about £500.'

Two public meetings held by the fledgling Swanage Railway Society in the summer of 1972 — while the track was being torn up — were to show the depth and strength of feeling against British Rail's actions and the support for a last-ditch effort to save and rebuild the Swanage branch line.

The first was held near London's Euston station on Monday 10 July 1972 — the day that track-lifting operations suddenly began at Corfe station. The meeting was greeted with scepticism by most members present from the defunct Isle of Purbeck Preservation Group but they were quickly converted to outright help. Support for the new Society also came

Above:
An historic day that will always stay in the minds of early Swanage Railway volunteers. On the morning of Saturday 14 February 1976, Swanage Railway Society swooped on the station like a plague of locusts — wrenching the boards off the windows to let the light in for the first time in three years, sweeping the platform and marking a start on restoring the rusting canopy outside the old parcels office and stationmaster's house. *Arthur Grant*

Right:

This is what the Swanage Railway Society members faced when they attended the first meeting at Swanage town hall on Saturday 5 August 1972. Looking towards the Railway Hotel and where the station stopblocks once stood, the one remaining track has been lifted and the sleepers wrenched from the ballast. The rails and track chairs dumped on the platform to await collection. The platform's enamel signs have not yet been removed.
Gerry Andrews

Below:

An Ivatt steam locomotive returns to Swanage for the first time since March 1967, and is seen here running round its train at Swanage station on Sunday 28 May 1989. No 46443 had just arrived with an afternoon train from Harman's Cross and Herston. Built in 1950, Ivatt 2-6-0 tender locomotive No 46443, spent her career working in the Midlands and was on loan to the Swanage Railway from the Severn Valley Railway.
Andrew P. M. Wright

from international film director, Bryan Forbes, and South Dorset MP, Evelyn King.

The second meeting of the new Swanage Railway Society was held in the Victorian splendour of Swanage's town hall on Saturday 5 August 1972. By then, the scrap merchants were well into dismantling Corfe station's passing loop — craning the rails on to a flat wagon and the bolts, chairs and fishplates into three open wagons.

'It was ironic that members of Swanage Urban District Council — including Arthur Gaskell, who'd spent over five years fighting the closure, were against the Swanage Railway Society,' Andrew explains. 'They seemed to feel that, as the guardians of the public interest, since they had failed to stop the closure and now the track-lifting, all hope was lost. They also felt that since they, the experts, had failed to stop the branch being lifted, a bunch of amateurs — most of whom then came from outside the area — couldn't possibly succeed.

'The protracted battle over Swanage station was one that we weren't really expecting to fight,' Andrew remembers. 'We found out that the large London firm of developers, Samuel Properties, were close to concluding negotiations with BR over the purchase of the station site. We went up to to see them but, of course, they said they weren't interested.'

It was while the station was under imminent threat of being flattened to make way for eight shops, a supermarket, public house, hotel, car park and service area that Sir John Betjemen agreed to be the patron of the new Society. Embarrassment was caused to the BR Property Board when South Dorset's MP, Evelyn King, wrote to Mr Lawrence bluntly asking why the board didn't offer the station to the highest bidder.

Ironically, it was the last desperate act of a dying council that ultimately saved Swanage's Victorian station. Local government reorganisation took effect from April Fool's Day 1974. It saw the old Swanage Urban District Council stripped of much of its power to become simply a town council, with the new Purbeck District Council having the upper hand throughout the area.

Just weeks before they became extinct, councillors on Swanage UDC voted to spend much of the Council's remaining balances in purchasing the four-and-a-half acre station site for £150,000 — quite a sum in 1972, when the average house cost around £18,000. However, after buying the site in the dying days of March 1974, the new town council dropped a bombshell on the Railway Society. It was revealed they would not lease them any part of the site, because the Council wanted

to use it as a 'green lung' recreational area for local people, complete with car park.

Instead, it was suggested the Society lease part of the county council owned trackbed on the Corfe side of the Northbrook Road bridge — opposite the derelict engine shed and coaling dock — for a station. With the very real fear that the bulldozers would move in to demolish the station and goods shed completely, Andrew Goltz made an impassioned, eleventh hour plea to let the residents of the town decide the future of the Railway Society through a referendum.

But, it was to take exactly one year for the town council to be finally persuaded — and embarrassed — into holding a referendum among the 8,500 residents of Swanage. In January 1975, Dorset County Council's planning and transportation committee voted to recommend the granting of a lease to the Swanage Railway Society for the quarter-mile stretch of trackbed from Northbrook Road to Victoria Avenue. Local residents, whose houses overlooked the abandoned trackbed, were none too pleased — objecting on the grounds of noise, fumes, general nuisance and the claim that the Society was 'doing nothing for Swanage'.

After Swanage's county councillor, Brigadier Ronald Montague-Jones, spoke strongly in favour of the Swanage Railway Society and its aims, the full council later ratified the committee's decision. However, the council threatened to withdraw the operating licence if a full amenity train service was not in operation between Swanage and Wareham by 1980.

So, in the summer of 1975 — while Britain was embroiled in voting on whether or not the country should stay in Europe — the worthy residents of Swanage were voting on a rather different issue; and one that could have killed the railway stone dead. Should the Railway Society be given the lease of the redundant station?

The deadline for voting was Monday 7 July 1975. Both sides waited nervously for the results as the ballot boxes were guarded by Town Clerk Alan Tootell who proudly described the referendum as being 'democracy with a capital "D"'. It seemed like something straight out of a quaint 1940s Ealing comedy film. The result of the poll was a resounding victory for the Swanage Railway Society with a tidal wave of support. A massive 83% of the votes cast were in favour of a rebuilt railway at Swanage station. Out of 233 postal votes, 174 wanted the railway back and just 59 did not.

History was made on Friday 13 February 1976, when the Swanage Railway Society sat round the table with the town council and signed their new one-year lease. It cost the

Above:

By the end of July 1972, the scrapmen from Eagre & Co of Scunthorpe lifting the track from Swanage had reached Woodyhyde Farm, between Harman's Cross and Corfe Castle. Looking towards Harman's Cross, work has started at bridge No 21 with the keys already knocked out of the chairs and the screws securing the chairs to the sleepers removed. Rails were next crowbarred out of the chairs and dragged by tractor to collection points at farm crossings. JCBs then moved in to wrench the sleepers out of the ballast. *Gerry Andrews*

Above right:

Swanage Railway staff work on rebuilding bridge No 21 on Thursday 15 March 1990. The rotting timbers of the old bridge can be seen in the foreground with the new deep piles and raft structure behind. Thanks to a special design by BR ex-Southern Region bridges inspector Bill Nobes — and special girders acquired from BR's Network SouthEast — the new bridge was of a hi-tech 'raft' design. Using deep piles, the weight of trains is taken by the piles and not the old Victorian bridge. Three such bridges costing a total of £50,000 had to be installed between Harman's Cross and Corfe Castle. *Andrew P. M. Wright*

enthusiasts £500. The following day — a Saturday morning — jubilant volunteers finally gained entry to the boarded-up station wielding brushes and screwdrivers, and carrying pots of paint.

In 1974, the Southern Steam Group came into existence with the intention of providing the Southern Railway hardware for the rebuilt Swanage branch — everything from locomotives to carriages and track materials. It became an educational Trust with charitable status in 1977.

Once the volunteers had received their first one-year lease, they had another battle in trying to get the town council to allow them to lay track out of the goods shed and back into the main platform, which they had dug out. Andrew Goltz recalls:

'We reasoned that as we tidied up and restored the station — with no security of tenure beyond the end of the lease — it would prove our credibility. Then, we could ask for a bit more, then a bit more and gradually move forward. As we restored the buildings and started to bring stock to the station, it was easier to sell the concept of a restored Swanage Railway because there was something on the ground to show people. Before 1976, it had just been talk and abstract ideas.

'By 1978, the volunteers were getting impatient to form a company and start to run public trains,' says Andrew. 'They wanted their own board of directors, which horrified me at the time because of the very fragile political position that the railway was still in.'

Ultimately, it was a difference of opinion and natural evolution within the volunteer-run organisation that caused Andrew Goltz and John Sloboda to leave the railway, as it developed growing pains. 'We'd laid tracks up to

Victoria Avenue, which was only a third of a mile from Herston. Whatever my personal doubts about the political maturity of the people on the new Swanage Railway Company Board, they were achieving the stage-by-stage negotiation and reconstruction that I'd proposed back in 1972, so I couldn't criticise.'

But, basic and irreconcilable differences of opinion came to a head at the Swanage Railway Society's 1978 annual general meeting. By the end of the meeting, the Society had been wound up and merged into the Swanage & Wareham Railway Group.

In order to try and achieve a rail link with the BR network at Furzebrook, Andrew Goltz decided to 'disguise' the project in order to protect its aims. Instead of a standard gauge link, a proposed narrow gauge railway for Purbeck was announced to shocked members at the AGM.

'We thought a narrow gauge railway would be cheaper and quicker to build, be seen less as a threat — and promote a less hostile attitude from central government and local authorities, whilst still delivering a public amenity service. In hindsight, I realise that I was slowly losing touch. Members greeted the proposals with horror — something that I really wasn't expecting.'

With the sharp difference between the founders of the Swanage Railway Society and its growing membership, Andrew Goltz and John Sloboda took stock of the situation and decided to leave the railway.

'Tendering my resignation was a bitter-sweet experience but I realised that what the railway project needed was a flatter, more concessionary style of management structure. I had run things on rather autocratic lines, because that's what was needed in 1972, when the track was being ripped up and everyone thought the Society's plans were a total impossibility.

'Even in the darkest days of 1972 I was always sure that the Swanage Railway would eventually achieve its aims. I had a fanatical zeal. The Society just kept on going, no matter what disaster befell us. The strange thing, looking back, is that after each setback had knocked the organisation down, it seemed to get back up stronger than it was before — no matter what the issues.

'But, looking back, I have nothing but admiration for what the Swanage Railway has achieved in the years since I left the project. I'm proud to have been associated with the railway at its birth and during its earliest years. I'll always look back to those times as being a most interesting and very rewarding part of my life.

'I could have handled people more sensitively but I was very green and rather arrogant then. You could call it youthful inexperience. Sometimes, a chirpy 22-year-old student, who's certain he's right, is not the best person to talk to a retired councillor or middle-aged BR official. I learnt through bitter experience and through my mistakes.'

Below left:
By the first week of August 1972, the workmen from Eagre & Co had lifted the 12-coach passing loop at Corfe Castle station. In this view taken from the Wareham end point looking towards Swanage, the rusty rails lifted from the loop wait to be collected and the sleepers dug up by a JCB. Work then began on dismantling the 'down' line. The rodding run to the left controlled the points and connected with the signalbox on the 'up' platform.
Gerry Andrews

Below:
Local people take the chance to walk the trackbed at Corfe Castle for the last time on the sunny evening of Thursday 27 September 1990, as the tracks are slowly relaid. Looking towards Swanage, work on laying the Wareham end point is well advanced. The passing loop still waits to be laid past the 'up' starter signal by the ex-Southern Railway 15-ton diesel crane built in 1947 for work at Southampton Docks.
Andrew P. M. Wright

The Prodigal Fireman's Tale

'Getting back on the footplate of an ex-BR main line steam locomotive was beyond belief — a real dream come true. If you'd told me when I left in 1960 that I'd be firing a "T9" and a Bulleid Pacific again in 1991, I'd have laughed in your face.'

Paul McDonald

One morning in Coronation year, 1953, 12-year-old Paul McDonald was stung by his teacher's steadfast refusal to allow him to look out of the classroom window. A pupil at Poole's Henry Harbin school, which overlooked the busy main London to Weymouth line, Paul used to love watching the maroon splendour of the 'Pines Express' as it thundered past in a dramatic cloud of smoke and steam en route for Bath and Manchester.

Thirty-eight years later the tables have been turned and the watcher has become the watched. It is a summer afternoon at Swanage station as LSWR 'T9' class 4-4-0 locomotive No 120 simmers at the head of her four-coach train. Clustered around her gleaming green livery and classic Victorian lines are tourists and railway enthusiasts. The volunteer guard glances at his watch and fiddles with his green flag.

The volunteer driver chats to the guard. Paul McDonald carefully shovels coal into the firebox and keeps a discerning eye on the pressure gauge. He checks the water levels in the glasses before the departure for Harman's Cross. Looking at his watch, Paul sits down on the fireman's seat and pours himself a cup of stewed tea from his white enamel can. Glancing up, he sees a youngster peering into the cab and smiles.

For Paul McDonald — a Swanage builder, engineer and musician — firing the 'T9' is definitely a feeling of *déjà vu*. Thirty-three years before, he was doing exactly the same thing — but on a much larger scale as a young fireman with British Railways at its Bournemouth depot. The wheel has now turned full circle.

'It really was a madhouse,' says Paul grinning as his mind goes back to the mid-1950s. 'Being a locomotive cleaner at Bournemouth shed was a cross between being at school and down a coal mine. I don't know how on earth we got away with some of the things we did.

'I can still smell the atmosphere at Bournemouth — with its blend of hot steam, warm lubricating oil, smoke, coal dust and general must. It was boiling on a hot summer's day and depressing on a damp winter's day.'

But, even in the early 1950s, Paul never thought that he would one day work on the locomotives that he idealised so much — the unrebuilt Bulleid Pacific; the 'West Country', the 'Battle of Britain' and the 'Merchant Navy' classes.

'It wasn't until a few weeks before I was due to leave school in the summer of 1956 that I thought seriously about joining British Railways. I left school in July 1956, about three or four weeks before my 15th birthday, and had written a letter to Mr Pringle, the shed foreman at Bournemouth depot, asking for a job. He wrote back asking me to come and see him.

'Looking back, it took some guts to see him, because he was a tall, thin man and very imposing and rather frightening to most people — let alone a 14-year-old boy. He told

me to go to Eastleigh for a medical and then come back. That I did and passed before going back to Mr Pringle.'

In an instant, Paul left the innocence of childhood behind him and was pitched headlong into the adult world of work — and the unique, bizarre and grimy world of the steam railway.

'Although not the size of Nine Elms or the other big London railway depots, Bournemouth was still impressive. There was the cleaning gang, the turning gang and then the old man's gang for pick-up goods work and station shunting. Further on, above that, was the junior and senior goods gang, the push-and-pull gang, or the "lug-and-shove" and then the three main line links.'

On his first day, Paul and the other new cleaners presented themselves to Tom Glassey, the cleaning foreman at Bournemouth.

'Tom was a real character,' remembers Paul with a grin. 'He knew every trick in the book and kept us cleaners in check. He was cunning but a real gent. I can still remember his call that used to echo round the sheds, "Come on then lads. Let's be havin' you, me boys".'

Paul was presented with a set of overalls which were four sizes too big and so long that he had to turn up the bottom of the trousers. Later, Paul and the rest of the lads would drain-pipe the trousers of their overalls so as to be trendy in the style of the mid-1950s.

'We were given a bundle of wipers and a flare lamp and told which engines we had to clean. My first weekly wage packet was five pounds and one shilling. Four of us would do a tender engine and two a tank. It was when I became a cleaner at Bournemouth that I got to know Alan Mabey. He went to the same school as me but was in the next year up. Starting a few days before me, he left BR at the same time I did. We're now both volunteers on the Swanage Railway. He's a cleaner and I'm a fireman.'

Being a cleaner with British Railways did have its advantages, despite the working conditions and the sheer physical strength and stamina needed to get the job done.

'We'd work like hell to clean the engine in the first few hours and then spend the rest of the day either playing cards in the smokebox of a locomotive, having a fight with oily rags, trying to throw buckets of water over one another or playing with the long leather hoses in the sheds. It was absolute bedlam, when I think of some of the crazy things we did as cleaners. Talk about youthful high spirits and exuberance, I'm really surprised no one got hurt.'

'The drivers' cabin was notorious for its filth and atmosphere. It had a fireplace with a roaring fire in one corner, scrubbed wooden tables and benches. The smell of smoke, water, tobacco and oil hung everywhere. There was always a card school going on there.

'Next door to the machine shop were the stores. To a 15-year-old boy, it was an absolutely wonderful place with all its brand-new spares for the locomotives; lubricators, whistles and injectors all lined up on racks. There was a long line of huge drums of locomotive engine oil down one side of the storeroom. Around the corner, out of sight, was a range on which staff used to cook delicious bacon

Right:

Another world of tradition and hierarchy now long gone. In the final months of steam, fireman Malcolm Collop climbs into the cab of rebuilt 'West Country' Bulleid Pacific No 34004 *Yeovil* by the coaling stage at Bournemouth MPD. A regular performer on the Swanage branch, No 34004 looks in a sorry state with her nameplate already removed. *Yeovil* hauled one of the final steam through trains to London from Swanage in September 1966, and the second last BR steam train of all to Corfe Castle and Swanage on Sunday 11 June 1967. *Mike Esau*

Below:

For Malcolm Collop, the thrill of firing and driving a main line steam locomotive didn't end with the death of BR Southern Region steam on Monday 10 July 1967. In the late 1980s, he joined the Swanage Railway and is seen here on the footplate of Victorian LSWR 'T9' class 4-4-0 No 120 with fireman Paul McDonald who cleaned and fired the 'T9s' at Bournemouth over 30 years before. Built in 1899, No 120 worked out of Bournemouth and down to Corfe Castle and Swanage from World War 1 until 1960.
Andrew P. M. Wright

and eggs. As I'd pass the hatch in the early morning, the smell of these bacon and eggs frying away on the stove used to drive me mad. Many's the time I befriended the store-man and sat there by the range during a night shift.

'Going out of the shed, you reached the cabin for the boiler washout men and the fire-lighters. They were real characters and used to wear leather and wooden clogs complete with horseshoe-type soles. It was all very archaic. I can remember going into their mess-room and talking with some of the old guys. They used to put thick Carnation tinned milk into their stewed tea.

'The sheds could be boiling in summer and freezing in winter — especially with a biting easterly wind blowing in across the yard. The worst memory I have is of throwing out the fire and disposing of a "Lord Nelson" loco-motive on a hot summer day. It was hell — beyond belief — and extremely hard work for a 16 or 17-year-old lad. Several cleaners passed out because of the heat.'

Always a music fan, Paul used to bring the hits of the mid-1950s to the darkest nooks and crannies of the steam sheds. 'A popular tune at that time was Tommy Steele's *Singing the Blues*. I'd be singing that at the top of my voice wherever I was working — perched on the engines, beside them or under them. I'm sure the other staff thought I was mad — especially the older drivers and firemen.'

In the summer of 1957, Paul started his short firing career with British Railways. And he can still remember being examined before being passed out as a fireman.

'When I was in the "old man's gang" at Bournemouth — made up of drivers who'd come off the main line because of age or health reasons — I'd fire the branch clay train down to Wareham, Furzebrook, Eldon's Siding at Norden and run round the wagons in the passing loop at Corfe Castle station. We'd do it every afternoon without fail and one of my regular drivers was Wilf Selby, who lived at Hamworthy.

'I always remember Wilf because he always used to be completely covered in oil from head to toe — and he'd eat his sandwiches with the most filthy hands I've ever seen. He was a nice old boy to work with, although he did used to get nervous if he had a young cleaner on with him. One trick he used to have was to put his bicycle on the tender of the locomotive, so he could get home early.

'We used to take the Drummond "Black Motor" "700s" down the branch — I remember good old No 30695 — as well as the "T9s", the "Us", the "S15s" and sometimes the "M7s". I didn't really enjoy the clay runs down the branch because it was all stopping and starting and it didn't seem as though we were going anywhere — not like the main line or the "Old Road".

'Another problem with the Purbeck clay duty was that your driver was from the "old man's gang" and they could sometimes be a load of old women, which was frustrating for a young fireman. For example, I'd be asked to clean the fire at Wareham instead of when we got back to Bournemouth.'

On one occasion in the late 1950s, Paul was put on loan to Swanage shed for the day and worked with the legendary senior branch driver, Jack 'Jock' Spicer. 'Jack was a real character. I think his regular fireman on the branch was off sick or had a rest day, so I was sent down from Bournemouth to help him work a goods. I can recall he was so portly that he had to get on to the footplate of the locomotive by turning sideways and lifting up his stomach to get on. He really was a railwayman from the old school and seemed very old-fashioned to me — I think he started his career back in the 1920s.'

As well as working freight and clay trains down to Corfe Castle and Swanage, Paul also had the honour of firing a Bulleid Pacific from Bournemouth down to the Purbeck seaside town.

'They were marvellous machines — wonderful to fire and a pleasure to work on. As young firemen we were impressionable and wanted to work on the newly-rebuilt Bulleids. I'll always remember the smell of fresh paint, oil

Below left:
Swanage station's engine shed and empty turntable pit lie deep amongst the weeds and dwarfed by looming elm trees on Saturday 5 August 1972, as the one remaining track is torn up beside it. The final steam locomotive to use the shed after 81 years spent the night there on Saturday 3 September 1966, so it could work the first train of the day from Swanage the following morning. The engine shed originally had an arched entrance with doors but after repeated accidents with engines overrunning the turntable and hitting the building, it was rebuilt with a wooden lintel in 1959.
Gerry Andrews

Below:
Catching up on lost years and a surprise chance reunion after nearly 40 years between two ex-Swanage branch firemen. Ex-fireman and driver Fred Norman (right) meets one-time branch fireman Stan Brown (left) on Swanage station's turntable on Sunday 26 May 1991. Stan was visiting the Swanage Railway to see his old steed 'T9' class 'Greyhound' No 120 for the first time in over 30 years. Fred was by the restored engine shed and bumped into Stan while feeding a tradition from the past — the station's black railway cat, 'Ebenezer'.
Andrew P. M. Wright

Right:
Harman's Cross station — the first entirely new station to be built in Dorset for 50 years — takes shape on Thursday 26 March 1988, in this view looking towards Corfe Castle. During World War 2, this is where Doug Scott's driver suddenly leapt off the engine to go ferreting. Swanage Railway staff and volunteers had to contend with horrendous conditions during the construction of the two six-coach platforms and run-round loop. The muddy clay always seemed to be a problem — even in the summer. *Andrew P. M. Wright*

Below right:
With no sign of the quagmire of mud endured during the construction of Harman's Cross station, Great Western Railway 0-6-2T locomotive No 5619 waits to leave Harman's Cross with LSWR 'T9' class 4-4-0 No 120 and the 15.40 train to Swanage on Sunday 7 April 1991. Built at Swindon in 1925, No 5619 was on loan from the Telford Horsehay Steam Trust in Shropshire. Another GWR 0-6-2T, No 6695, is currently being restored to working condition at Swanage. *Andrew P. M. Wright*

Right:
A peaceful summer lunchtime at Corfe Castle station in 1964 — and a scene that many thought would last forever. Ex-LMS Ivatt 2-6-2T No 41312 simmers at the 'down' platform with the two-coach 12.26 train from Wareham to Swanage on Friday 12 June 1964. Maunsell coaches ran to Swanage until mid-1965 before being replaced with Bulleid coaches off the main line. Withdrawn in July 1967, No 41312 was rescued from the cutter's torch and is now preserved in Caerphilly, South Wales. *John Scrace*

Above left:
Corfe Castle station lies deserted and a haven for wildlife on the afternoon of Saturday 5 July 1986. Where passengers once swarmed off the train, country walkers occasionally amble along the weed-ridden platforms. In this view taken from the end-loading dock, the 'down' platform is completely hidden by choking undergrowth and the old wooden waiting shelter smothered in ivy and in danger of collapse.
Andrew P. M. Wright

Left:
A momentous piece of history took place when Swanage volunteers relaid the track through Corfe Castle's cleared and repaired platforms on the afternoon of Wednesday 5 September 1990. The choking undergrowth and weeds already a memory, ex-SR 15-ton diesel-electric crane gently lays a 60ft track panel as it steers clear of overhead telephone wires. The wooden waiting shelter on the 'down' platform is already restored to its former glory thanks to carpentry students from Weymouth College. *Andrew P. M. Wright*

Below left:
The wheel turns full circle. LSWR 'T9' 'Greyhound' class 4-4-0 No 120 from the National Railway Museum at York was the first ex-BR main line steam locomotive to steam into Corfe Castle station since Sunday 18 June 1967. On Friday 10 May 1991, No 120 gently runs into the 'down' platform with the Swanage Railway's Chief Mechanical Engineer, Martyn Ashworth, at the controls. The 'T9s' last visited Corfe Castle in the late 1950s on clay workings, goods trains and occasionally acted as station pilot at Swanage on busy summer Saturdays.
Andrew P.M Wright

119

and the new wooden floorboards in the cabs. Everything was new and spick and span.

'In contrast, the "T9s" and other locomotives of their generation were old hat and coming to the end of their lives and in quite a state. Then we didn't appreciate them — not like now.'

The peak of Paul's firing career — just before he left British Railways — was firing a rebuilt Bulleid Pacific from London Waterloo down to Bournemouth Central. Paul McDonald's memories are interrupted as "T9" No 30120 — on loan to the Swanage Railway from the National Railway Museum's collection — steams by just a few feet away on the other side of his garden fence with a packed five-coach train bound for Harman's Cross.

It was while working a goods train down to Swanage that Paul met a young girl who was to be his future wife — and the reason why he left the railways. 'I first met Vera during a rest break at Swanage when I went into the town's Woolworths store just a few yards down from the railway station. We used to meet on the station between trains.'

Paul left British Railways in late 1960 with two of his mates — including Alan Mabey, who is now a fellow volunteer on the Swanage Railway.

'We were young and we wanted to enjoy life. Alan Mabey and I used to race Swanage branch fireman, Keith Sloper, on his motorbike between Swanage and Wareham. We were mad then and into music, motorbikes and girls. While our mates were out enjoying themselves we were working shifts at all hours of the day and night, weekends and bank holidays.'

Paul has been back to the site of Bournemouth's steam sheds, which were unceremoniously demolished in late 1967. It is now an overspill car park. He admits that standing there, as hi-tech Class 442 'Wessex Electrics' whined past, was a strange experience.

'I've looked down from the Beechey Road bridge and stood where I used to work back in the fifties. Although all the memories came flooding back I couldn't believe it was the same spot. The 1950s seem a million years away. It was really weird — I couldn't see anything that's there now, which I recalled seeing then. They seem like two entirely different places.

'When the Swanage Railway ran their first trains in the summer of 1979, I couldn't get excited at the thought of firing an industrial steam engine over a hundred yards of track at Swanage — not after firing a Bulleid Pacific from Bournemouth to London. It was purely selfish, I admit that. But, I really admire what the volunteers have managed to achieve in the early days.

'It was when the Swanage Railway reached Harman's Cross and "Battle of Britain" Bulleid Pacific No 34072 *257 Squadron* and the "T9" were due to arrive that I realised if I didn't join the locomotive department, it would all sail past me and I would have missed being a part of it. I couldn't have forgiven myself if that had happened.

'I knew the Swanage Railway would get through in the end, because of my sheer passion and thrill for railways — and knowing what it does to people. It takes a grip of you and takes your life over — it really does. I cannot understand people who don't like railways. The public don't appreciate, or probably even realise, the sacrifices that the volunteers at Swanage have made — and are still making — to build and run the railway. I live next to the railway but I have difficulty in getting time off from the family to do the modest amount that I do. Some people must give their lives over to it. How they are there weekend after weekend is really beyond me.

'I find it very difficult to keep a balance. I struggle to do the little that I do on the railway, keep down my job and spend time with the family. Vera, my wife, hates me working on the railway because it takes me away from her. But, it's a continual challenge — something that I've got to do, because it's a part of me.

'But I do get a great buzz out of a 12-hour day on the footplate — when you are part of a good team and everything goes well — despite the work being physically tiring. At the end of a turn, even after only doing six or seven six-mile return trips up to Harman's Cross with five or six coaches on, I come home exhausted.

'Firing a temperamental steam locomotive is a challenge. I was rather apprehensive when I turned up for my first day's work on the "T9" and the unrebuilt Bulleid Pacific No 34072 *257 Squadron*, because I hadn't worked on steam engines for 30 years. Getting back on the footplates of those two machines was beyond belief — a real dream come true. If in 1960 you'd told me that I would be firing a "T9" and a Bulleid Pacific again in the 1990s, I would have laughed in your face.

'I'm still looking forward to firing and perhaps driving a steam locomotive to Corfe Castle and then on into Wareham station's north bay platform. That really would be marvellous — absolutely brilliant. If I get another 10 years on the Swanage Railway footplate I'll be a very happy man,' says Paul McDonald with a cheeky grin.

The Volunteer's Tale

'We all felt betrayed and very let down. After all the years of work and money that members had put in since 1972, we got to within a week of completely folding. It was sickening — we never thought it could or would happen to us.'

Peter Duncalfe

A young bank manager has a smile of self-satisfaction on his grimy face as he leans from the footplate of a huge, simmering Bulleid Pacific steam locomotive — waiting for the whistle and green flag from the guard as the last passengers scamper on board the train.

However, 15 years before, on Saturday 14 February 1976, it was a dramatically contrasting scene at Swanage station. Then, there was no simmering Bulleid Pacific, no coaches, no track and not even a platform. All that could be heard was the sound of nails and boards being wrenched off window frames, hand scrapers relentlessly stripping peeling paint and rust from the station canopy, and brooms brushing away four years of accumulated rubbish. In short, there was no railway at all — just boarded-up and rapidly deteriorating station buildings, a broad expanse of weed-infested ballast and a line of road coaches and beach pedal boats parked where trains once departed.

Peter Duncalfe, the driver and bank manager — envied and admired by the watching public in 1991 — was an enthusiastic but naive 14-year-old boy in 1976. Then, he was helping to strip age-stained wallpaper off the walls of the 'newly-liberated' stationmaster's house at Swanage.

By his very own admission, the Swanage Railway is a 'drug' and 'once you are hooked you can't get away'. But, at weekends and during valuable holidays he leaves the cosy confines of his Bournemouth bank and becomes a fully trained and qualified locomotive driver and member of the railway's permanent way track gang.

'My friends and I used to catch the bus from Wareham to school in Swanage every day during the early 1970s and I can remember we used to delay coming home on the first available bus, so we could go up and take a look at the old station. In its derelict state it really used to fascinate me.'

It was Peter and his school friends who first became involved with the Swanage Railway Society when it was given a one-year lease of the town's station in 1976 — after four years of fierce campaigning. Many of those friends are still with the railway in the 1990s, while others have moved away to follow careers and start families.

'I clearly remember that February day in 1976 when we gained access to the station. It was incredible to finally get there. I spent the day scraping wallpaper off the inside of the

Above:
The site of the Swanage Railway's first new halt at Herston on a winter's morning in 1977, looking along the weed-ridden trackbed under the Washpond Lane bridge towards Harman's Cross and Corfe Castle. The final BR train clattered through here five years before and the original track was lifted during the second week of July 1972. All the bridges along the branch were built to double-track width. *Peter Sykes*

Above right:
By 1990, Herston was the busiest it had ever been with trains passing at the small halt. On peak weekends, two trains have to be run from Swanage and Harman's Cross, passing at Herston Halt, to cope with public demand. GWR 0-6-2T No 5619 of 1925 waits in the loop with a train from Swanage to Harman's Cross on Sunday 1 April 1990, as Hunslet 'Austerity' 0-6-0ST *Whiston* of 1950 drifts into Herston Halt with the single-line staff and a train from Harman's Cross. *Andrew P. M. Wright*

stationmaster's house which was in a terrible state.'

But 14-year-old Peter's intentions to become actively involved, as the railway started from nothing, were rudely thwarted by some shattering news.

'I was bluntly told to go away and come back when I was 16 years of age because I was too young to work on the railway. After the euphoria of helping to clean up the station building, being told to go off for two years was like a kick in the teeth.'

However, such was Peter's determination to get involved with the embryonic railway that instead of walking off and finding something else to do with his spare time, the youngster waited until he reached his 16th birthday.

'I and my other friends watched the slow progress of the railway from the public side of the lineside fence. I was there to see items of stock and track — a petrol shunter, ex-BR Standard 4 tank No 80078, a GWR hand crane, a Bulleid carriage and two Southern Railway luggage vans — as they arrived at the station between 1976 and 1978. Every arrival was an important milestone. But, there was still no track to speak of, because the Swanage Town Council wouldn't allow us to lay it.'

When 1977 gave way to 1978, Peter started to count the months, then the weeks and finally the days to his 16th birthday when he would be able to help the railway on site.

'I didn't want it all to happen without me,' remembers Peter, 'and when I did turn 16 in October of that year, we were feverishly trying to lay a few hundred yards of track and restore a diesel shunter and a carriage to run the first passenger trains since 1972.

'A lot of people thought the railway would come to nothing. I have to say that in 1978, I thought we'd only get as far as Herston — one mile up the line. It seemed like a big mountain just to lay track by hand to get the half mile to the Victoria Avenue road bridge.

'There was a great deal of anti-railway feeling in Swanage during the middle to late 1970s. One member of our permanent way gang was assaulted, when a heavy lump hammer was thrown at him by an irate local resident who took exception to us relaying the line.'

Although rebuilding an entire and self-sufficient railway system from scratch has been difficult, uncomfortable, expensive and time-consuming, Peter still remembers the 'highs' experienced since 1976.

'Watching the first diesel train — comprising Fowler 250hp 0-4-0 shunter *May* and half-painted Bulleid carriage — run over just a few hundred yards of track in August 1979 was an incredible and tremendous feeling. We had actually achieved something from nothing — everything had been the result of our efforts.

'We charged 10p for a ticket then and my job on the first day was to make sure the public didn't fall off the temporary platform made of scaffolding. Then we used to ballast what little track we had by shovelling it into an old concrete-laying shoot before lifting it with a hand crane and then running up perhaps two hundred yards to the end of the line where we'd spread the ballast. That was hard work.

'Another memorable high was when we ran our first locomotive — a tiny petrol shunter from Corralls at Poole Quay — over just a panel of short track at Swanage in the summer of 1976. That was the first and only thing we had but it seemed the world that afternoon.'

Peter smiles when he recalls the volunteers' first experience of a steam engine — albeit a tiny oil-fired one.

'Andrew Barclay 0-4-0ST *Richard Trevithick* was our very first steam engine and arrived at Swanage in 1979 from Goldington power station, near Bedford. After firing her up with wood you had to flash her over to the oil burner. We did that, heard a great crashing and roaring sound from below the locomotive and all immediately jumped off the engine. It turned out the burner always made that sound when being fired up, but it gave us quite a fright.'

Other highs for Peter and his fellow volunteers included the completion of the track up to Harman's Cross station before the first test train in late 1988 as well as laying a mile of track from Woodyhyde, under the Afflington Bridge and over Corfe Common in just seven days during a concentrated 10-day work-in during April 1990.

'It was a terrific feeling of achievement to clear a length of trackbed that was choked with thick undergrowth and trees, so you could see the alignment of the trackbed for the first time since 1972. Then would begin the back-breaking work of "weeding" the ballast, laying the track and then ballasting and jacking and packing before the first train. Sometimes now it's hard to visualise how the line from Swanage to Harman's Cross looked before we started work.'

Rebuilding the Swanage Railway since 1976 has called for hard work, grinding determination and a clarity of purpose and vision from all the volunteers.

Above left:
With the Purbeck Hills and the new houses of Harman's Cross behind, the 10-coach 'Dorset Coast Express' railtour pounds up the 1 in 76 gradient between Quarr Farm and Harman's Cross with one of the final steam trains to visit Corfe Castle and Swanage on the afternoon of Sunday 7 May 1967. Organised by the Locomotive Club of Great Britain, the special ran from London and had BR Standard Class 4 tank No 80011 on the Wareham end, and unrebuilt 'West Country' Bulleid Pacific No 34023 *Blackmore Vale* at the other. Withdrawn in July 1967, No 34023 was saved from the scrapyard and is now located on the Bluebell Railway in Sussex. *Sid C. Nash*

Left:
Shades of the 1940s and 1950s and double-headed holiday trains running down to Corfe Castle and Swanage. Running in Purbeck for the first time since the late 1950s, 'T9' 'Greyhound' class 4-4-0 No 120 of 1899 pilots 1948-built 'Battle of Britain' class Bulleid Pacific No 34072 *257 Squadron* up the 1 in 76 to Harman's Cross station on Sunday 3 March 1991, with the seven-coach 14.30 train from Swanage. The Purbeck Hills are still visible but the houses of Harman's Cross are now hidden by 20 years worth of trees. *Andrew P. M. Wright*

123

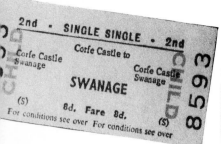

'You have to believe in what you're doing to get up at 3am for six consecutive Saturdays and travel from Wareham to the Isle of Grain in Essex and then spend the day carefully lifting half a mile of old track before bringing it back to Swanage.

'You've then got to store it in 60ft panels and then start all over again and lay it. We have done that for the whole three miles between Swanage and Harman's Cross. Before reaching Herston in 1983, we had to use an old GWR handcrane to lift the sleepers and rails before putting it all together by hand.

'The motivation as to why we battled away in the really early days — laying a few yards of track by hand, restoring a carriage and trying to restore an old diesel shunter — is one of those strange things to explain. It was born out of frustration. There was a railway the Purbecks needed that had been closed and we were being prevented from rebuilding it. We were indignant that it could pay — I suppose we were all righting a tremendous wrong that had been perpetrated in 1972.

'I can remember digging out the coal dock and engine pit at Swanage on that weekend in February 1976. The only tools we had were a pickaxe, a shovel and an old wheelbarrow. If you had told us then that we could have re-created anything from that moonscape at the station, we would have laughed in your face — it was total pie in the sky, even to us committed volunteers.

'But, the enthusiasm was there right from the start and it drew together a group of like-minded people of all ages and from all walks of life. It was quite incredible looking back.

'I now get a tremendous kick out of driving a steam locomotive. It is really hard work and, despite the 12 or 14-hour days, I get a real thrill from it. That's even when I have spent a day on the footplate, before shovelling one-and-a-half tons of coal into the tender and disposing of the engine at the end of a working day. With a steam locomotive you have complete and utter control. If you and your fireman aren't doing your jobs properly, then you just don't go anywhere. As a driver you make a steam locomotive live. I know it's a well-worn cliche but it's true — it really is.

'The Swanage Railway — even in times of crisis or under pressure — is like a big extended family with everyone helping each other.'

That was to prove very true when the Swanage Railway's toughest test in its eventful history took place in March 1991, with the resignation of the Project's General Manager and Finance Director, Mel Norris. Members were shocked and appalled to be told by volunteers, on an officially appointed emergency manage-

Above right:
Waiting to depart with a train for London Waterloo, Bournemouth Driver Stan Symes oils the motion of a rebuilt 'West Country' class Bulleid Pacific at Swanage station's main platform in the summer of 1966. Just 20 years later he would be back at Swanage, driving steam trains as a volunteer. Stan's trademark was the North American driver's cap he always wore — a souvenir of the four months he spent as a fireman on Canadian National Railways and a boilersmith's mate on the Canadian Pacific Railway in 1952. *Chris Phillips*

Right:
Times don't change at Swanage. 25 years after Stan Symes stood on the same spot to oil a huge Bulleid Pacific — like generations of railwaymen before him — the Swanage Railway's Chief Mechanical Engineer, Martyn Ashworth, oils up LSWR 'T9' 'Greyhound' class 4-4-0 No 120 before departing with the 15.40 train for Harman's Cross on Saturday 22 June 1991. Martyn has worked in locomotive engineering and on preserved railways around the country since a teenager — but few are aware that he also has a sociology degree. *Andrew P. M. Wright*

ment committee, that the Swanage Railway had allegedly amassed nearly £500,000 worth of debts and liabilities — teetering on the edge of complete bankruptcy.

'We went to within one week of completely folding. We'd been through so much to get as far as we had — how could this have happened under our noses?' recalls Peter soberly. 'We all felt betrayed and very, very let down after all the years and the money that members had put in since 1972. It was utterly sickening — the nightmare scenario, I suppose, which we all feared at the back of our minds but we never thought it could or would happen to us.'

When the financial crisis exploded, then Southern Steam Trust Chairman, Mike Stollery, admitted to shocked members that the Purbeck Line 'has been suffering its most traumatic period of its existence, culminating in the full realisation of the extent of the mismanagement, which brought the Swanage Railway to near ruin'.

He admitted that the long list of outstanding creditors was 'horrendous'. There was a loan-guarantee from Dorset County Council of £250,000 secured against railway assets of over £1 million, an operating company overdraft in excess of £80,000 and a list of creditors that passed the £120,000 mark.

'You can have an authentic and atmospheric preserved railway, a worthwhile public transport link, an enthusiastic volunteer staff backed up by a small core of full-timers — and a healthy tourist business. There is no contradiction there, as the Keighley & Worth Valley Railway in West Yorkshire has proved by achieving the right balance.

'The biggest mistake you can make is to regard the Swanage Railway as just a life-size train set. It isn't — it's a living and breathing business that will soon have a £1 million annual turnover and has responsibilities to its volunteers and the general community.

'The trouble with the Swanage Railway — and all independent railways that have started from scratch — is that the very enthusiasm, blind faith and commitment that started them in the beginning is often their worst enemy as they grow and struggle to mature.

'The Swanage Railway is and has always been, even from the earliest days, a broad church with a wide range of people, skills, interests and points of view. That's what makes it so alive. The financial crisis, the resulting investigation and re-structuring was a valuable chance to make the volunteer management and any full-time staff accountable to members on the ground.

'In retrospect, and with the benefit of hindsight, the Swanage Railway's great mistake

was getting to Corfe Castle at any cost and gambling on the extension opening in 1991. We overstretched ourselves — conquering the physical challenge but not the monetary one.

'The financial problems of 1991 will delay the railway's plans by two or three years. Strange as it may seem, I think we'll open to Corfe Castle at the same time had we slowly rebuilt the three underbridges and laid the extension to Corfe slowly — consolidating as we went.

'We owe a lot to many people that are no longer with the railway. If it hadn't been for the determination and stubbornness of Andrew Goltz, then the seed of the Swanage Railway wouldn't have even been planted; and if it hadn't been for our first volunteer operations manager, Geoff Pitman, banging heads together back in 1979, then we wouldn't have reached Herston and completed that first mile of track.

'But, there are other people, too. The late John Clothier was our first locomotive superintendent, when we got our first diesel shunter and steam locomotives. He taught us a tremendous amount. Then, there was Dave Ford, who tragically died of cancer in November 1990.

'A keen volunteer, he did a tremendous amount to help both the Swanage Railway and the Port Line Project. Dave was my regular fireman and was the best we had on the railway. He was with me on the footplate when taken ill and yet he continued to work until a few days before his death — helping to lay track at Corfe Castle station.

Below:
Marooned on her road transporter on Friday 26 May 1989, the Swanage Railway's most powerful diesel locomotive runs over the A351 Afflington road bridge — under which she will be running en route to Corfe Castle — en route to her new home at Swanage. The ex-BR 74-tonne Sulzer-powered Class 25 diesel-electric locomotive No 25244 was built at Darlington in 1964. Working throughout the country, she covered a working mileage of a million miles before being withdrawn in 1986. *Andrew P. M. Wright*

Right:
The track under the A351 Afflingon road bridge on the southern approach to Corfe Castle waits to be lifted during the second week of July 1972. The scrap merchants, Eagre & Co of Scunthorpe, have already undone the screws securing the chairs. The rails wait to be crowbarred out of the chairs, which will then be thrown to the side of the trackbed and the wooden sleepers dug up with a JCB.
Gerry Andrews

Far right:
The spirit of the Swanage Railway. Permanent way volunteers Tony Bray from Portsmouth (left) and Wayne Masters from Poole (right) take a break from the back-breaking work of clearing 17 years worth of choking undergrowth and trees from the Afflington cutting in February 1989. Thanks to their determined work, the A351 Afflington road bridge has become visible for the first time. *Andrew P. M. Wright*

Bottom right:
Eighteen years after watching the track that he helped maintain torn up for scrap, BR track worker and Swanage Railway volunteer Tony Trood, from Wareham, helps relay it in 1990. During tracklaying on Tuesday 10 April 1990, Tony (left) and fellow volunteer Andy Tidby, from Ringwood in Hampshire, found chair bolts left by the scrap merchants from the original BR track.
Andrew P. M. Wright

'And, of course, there was the late John Herring, who worked for London Transport and helped us obtain our first track and sleepers in 1978 and 1979 — and acquired our turntable from Neasden in 1980. Without volunteers, who poured themselves into the Swanage Railway for no personal gain, the Purbeck Line wouldn't have got out of the station at Swanage.

'In 1979, when we ran the first train over 200 yards of track from a temporary scaffolding platform under Northbrook Bridge, we were 90% enthusiasm and 10% skill. Ten years later, the position was reversed with 80% skill and 20% enthusiasm.

'The Swanage Railway will achieve its aims. I'm certain of that. It will just take longer than anticipated, but that's always been the way throughout our history. After the financial crisis, we just had to knuckle down and get on with the job ourselves.'

Support and encouragement has come from no less than British Rail itself. In a letter to the Swanage Railway Company's then volunteer chairman, David Cash, the high-powered director of BR Network SouthEast, Chris Green, praised the volunteers for the huge amount that they had been able to achieve since 1972. And the man in charge of one of the world's most intensive railway systems made it clear that a link between the two railways could only be good — for everyone in the community.

'You are performing miracles as you narrow the gap between Harman's Cross and Furzebrook,' he told the volunteers after a fact-finding visit in December 1989.

'My overriding impression is one of professional teamwork by people who are enjoying their work. My visit reconfirmed my belief that the greatest commercial benefit for both parties now lies in a steam operation into the "up" bay platform at Wareham,' he added.

Peter Duncalfe is keen to emphasise that the Swanage Railway is not immune from change, but that it must not forget its roots and how it started.

'The euphoria of reaching Harman's Cross in 1989 and opening the new station there — as well as receiving the support and goodwill of the local authorities and British Rail — probably lulled us into a false sense of security and clouded our judgement.

'A hard core of volunteers have sacrificed more than they'd probably care to admit. It's quite incredible how the "social club", the "toy railway" of 1979 and Sunday afternoon "hobby" has undergone a metamorphosis to now be a fully fledged, running railway with a purpose and a direction. And it all came out of nothing.

'I'll be with the Swanage Railway until I drop,' admits Peter. 'It's in my blood and there's nothing I can do about it. It is like a drug — once you are hooked, you can't get away. I do what I do for no personal gain — like the other volunteers down here — but simply because I believe in the Swanage Railway and what it has and is still trying to achieve.'

Just some of the men and women that make the Swanage Railway run — and push it still further towards a long-awaited connection with British Rail. The permanent way department pauses for a rest in the sun between bouts of track-laying at Afflington on Monday 9 April 1990, before pushing on still closer to Corfe Castle. From there it's just one-and-a-half miles to the BR system at Norden where Purbeck's railway will once again be completed.
Andrew P. M. Wright

Rear cover, top:
Suffocated under 17 years of choking undergrowth, a decaying Corfe station sleeps below the massive ruins of the Medieval castle as the disused branch line awaits the Swanage Railway's track relaying train one summer morning in 1989. With the last BR train clattering through the Isle of Purbeck on the dark evening of New Year's Day 1972, the track between Furzebrook and Swanage was ripped up for scrap during July and August, 1972. It is hard to believe but just 22 years before this picture was taken the rural peace of Corfe station was shattered by the 10-coach 'Dorset Coast Express' railtour of Sunday 7 May 1967 — only weeks before the end of all BR steam traction in Dorset.
John Spencer-Gilks/Ryedale AV

Rear cover, bottom:
With the excitement and splendour of the 'Dorset Coast Express' railtour of 1967 just a memory, Swanage Railway volunteers triumphantly relay their tracks into Corfe Castle station in August 1990 — 18 years since the tracks were ripped up and nature made its remorseless comeback. It was a cherished and heartfelt dream come true after years of fighting hard to relay the Swanage branch line after closure by British Rail in 1972. *Andrew P. M. Wright*